Student Activity Guide for

Working with Young Children

by

Dr. Judy Herr
Professor, Early Childhood Development
College of Human Development
University of Wisconsin-Stout
Menomonie, Wisconsin

Publisher
The Goodheart-Willcox Company, Inc.
Tinley Park, Illinois

Introduction

This activity guide is designed for use with the text *Working with Young Children*. It will help you recall, review, and expand on the concepts presented in the text. It will also help you understand how to meet children's developmental needs as you teach and care for them.

The best way to use this activity guide is to begin by reading your assignment in the text. You will find that the activities in the activity guide correspond to the chapters in the text. Follow the instructions carefully at the beginning of each activity.

You will find a variety of activities in this guide. Some activities, such as true/false and matching activities, review text information. These can be used as study guides as you review in preparation for quizzes and tests. Do your best to complete these activities carefully and accurately. Try to complete as much of each activity as you can without referring to the text. Then compare the answers you have to the information in *Working with Young Children*. At that time you can also complete any questions you could not answer.

Other activities will ask for your ideas, opinions, evaluations, and conclusions that cannot be judged as right or wrong. The object of these activities is to encourage you to consider alternatives and evaluate situations thoughtfully. The text will be a useful reference in completing these activities.

The activities in this guide have been designed to be both interesting and fun to do. This activity guide will help you apply what you have learned as you work with children now and in the future.

International Standard Book Number 1-56637-823-0
1 2 3 4 5 6 7 8 9 10   02 07 06 05 04 03 02 01

Contents

Part Two
Creating a Safe and Healthy Environment

Part Three
Guiding Children

Part Four
Learning Experiences for Children

Part Five
Other People You Will Meet

You: Working with Young Children

Truths About Early Childhood

Activity A

Chapter 1

Name _____

Date _____ Period_____

Read the following statements. Circle *T* if the statement is true or *F* if the statement is false.

T   F   1.   Early childhood covers the period from birth to nine years of age.

T   F   2.   Social and economic changes will continue to create a need for more child care services.

T   F   3.   Fewer than half of all preschool children are in child care arrangements.

T   F   4.   The number of single parent families has decreased since 1960.

T   F   5.   Corporate-sponsored child care will continue to grow in the future.

T   F   6.   Companies have found that providing child care has a negative effect on morale and absenteeism.

T   F   7.   There are more opportunities in early childhood now than ever before.

T   F   8.   Full-day kindergartens are increasing in number.

T   F   9.   In the future, there will most likely be a greater allocation of public education dollars for early childhood.

T   F   10.   Nannies work in their own homes to care for children.

T   F   11.   An au pair is a person from a foreign country who provides child care.

T   F   12.   Kindergarten teachers only work in public schools.

T   F   13.   A child care director recruits children, hires and supervises staff, and manages the budget.

T   F   14.   The teacher in a child care center has broader responsibilities than the director.

T   F   15.   Licensing specialists are employed by the state to ensure that state rules and regulations are followed.

T   F   16.   Parent educators may design written materials to help parents better understand their roles and the nature of young children.

T   F   17.   To be a teacher's aide, a person needs an associate degree.

T   F   18.   To obtain the CDA Credential, you must take courses in child care education.

Comparing Teaching to Other Careers

Name _____

Date _____ Period_____

Before making a career choice, you should compare several careers. In the chart below, use descriptive phrases to show how teaching compares in each area with another career that interests you.

CATEGORY	TEACHING	CAREER: _____
Preparation and education required		
Primary job responsibilities		
Workplace environment		
Pay		
Relationships with coworkers		
Communication skills needed		
Time management skills needed		
Continuing education suggested		
Satisfaction gained from career		

Pleasures and Problems in Teaching

Activity C

Chapter 1

Name _____

Date _____ Period_____

Listed below are typical activities of early childhood teachers. Read the activities and indicate whether you feel each activity would be pleasant, unpleasant, or if you are unsure.

Pleasant	Unpleasant	Unsure		
_____	_____	_____	1.	Rocking children to sleep.
_____	_____	_____	2.	Meeting new parents.
_____	_____	_____	3.	Changing diapers.
_____	_____	_____	4.	Teaching children to dress themselves.
_____	_____	_____	5.	Writing parent letters.
_____	_____	_____	6.	Selecting new equipment.
_____	_____	_____	7.	Reading stories.
_____	_____	_____	8.	Helping children cope with fears.
_____	_____	_____	9.	Comforting sad children.
_____	_____	_____	10.	Teaching songs to children.
_____	_____	_____	11.	Designing bulletin boards.
_____	_____	_____	12.	Arranging the classroom.
_____	_____	_____	13.	Selecting art activities.
_____	_____	_____	14.	Attending conferences.
_____	_____	_____	15.	Reading articles on child growth and development.
_____	_____	_____	16.	Settling disputes between children.
_____	_____	_____	17.	Taking field trips.
_____	_____	_____	18.	Telling puppet stories.
_____	_____	_____	19.	Wiping up spills.
_____	_____	_____	20.	Coping with temper tantrums.
_____	_____	_____	21.	Planning holiday parties.
_____	_____	_____	22.	Teaching safety.
_____	_____	_____	23.	Planning nutritious meals and snacks.
_____	_____	_____	24.	Laughing with children.
_____	_____	_____	25.	Recording children's progress.

List the activities that you would consider most pleasant and explain why.

_____

_____

_____

_____

_____

(Continued)

List the activities that you would consider most unpleasant.

_____

_____

_____

_____

_____

_____

_____

Review your responses. Do you feel certain or uncertain about becoming an early childhood teacher? For what reasons do you feel this way?

_____

_____

_____

_____

_____

_____

Characteristics for Working with Children

Activity D

Chapter 1

Name _____

Date _____ Period _____

People who enjoy working with young children tend to have certain characteristics in common. Many of these characteristics are listed below. For each of the characteristics, rate yourself as **(S)** strong, **(A)** average, or **(W)** weak. Then have a family member or friend rate you on the same set of characteristics using the form on the following page.

_____ Active	_____ Humorous
_____ Affectionate	_____ Intelligent
_____ Alert	_____ Kind
_____ Ambitious	_____ Levelheaded
_____ Artistic	_____ Likable
_____ Broad-minded	_____ Nurturing
_____ Calm	_____ Organized
_____ Capable	_____ Patient
_____ Careful	_____ Practical
_____ Competent	_____ Realistic
_____ Considerate	_____ Resourceful
_____ Cooperative	_____ Responsible
_____ Creative	_____ Self-controlled
_____ Dependable	_____ Sensible
_____ Eager	_____ Serious
_____ Efficient	_____ Sincere
_____ Energetic	_____ Stable
_____ Enthusiastic	_____ Thorough
_____ Firm	_____ Tolerant
_____ Flexible	_____ Understanding
_____ Friendly	_____ Warm
_____ Healthy	_____ Well-groomed
_____ Honest	_____ Wholesome

Write in additional characteristics that you feel should describe someone who works with young children. Also rate yourself in those areas.

_____ _____

_____ _____

_____ _____

_____ _____

_____ _____

(Continued)

Name _____

In the space below, have a family member or friend rate you as **(S)** strong, **(A)** average, or **(W)** weak for each characteristic.

_____ Active		_____ Humorous
_____ Affectionate		_____ Intelligent
_____ Alert		_____ Kind
_____ Ambitious		_____ Levelheaded
_____ Artistic		_____ Likable
_____ Broad-minded		_____ Nurturing
_____ Calm		_____ Organized
_____ Capable		_____ Patient
_____ Careful		_____ Practical
_____ Competent		_____ Realistic
_____ Considerate		_____ Resourceful
_____ Cooperative		_____ Responsible
_____ Creative		_____ Self-controlled
_____ Dependable		_____ Sensible
_____ Eager		_____ Serious
_____ Efficient		_____ Sincere
_____ Energetic		_____ Stable
_____ Enthusiastic		_____ Thorough
_____ Firm		_____ Tolerant
_____ Flexible		_____ Understanding
_____ Friendly		_____ Warm
_____ Healthy		_____ Well-groomed
_____ Honest		_____ Wholesome

How would the characteristics in which you are strong benefit you in a career working with young children?

_____

_____

_____

_____

What actions can you take to strengthen the areas in which you are weak?

_____

_____

_____

_____

Types of Early Childhood Programs

Early Childhood Fill-In

Activity A

Chapter 2

Name _____

Date _____ Period_____

Based on information in the text, complete each of the following sentences by writing the correct word or words in the blanks on the left.

_____ 1. Most parents who enroll children in a full-day program are highly influenced by the _____ of the program.

_____ 2. _____ allow children to go to their homes after school and receive calls from caregivers to be sure there are no problems.

_____ 3. _____ in Montessori schools involve learning to button, zip, tie, and put on coats and boots.

_____ 4. Some companies provide a _____ service that matches the parents' needs with specific centers.

_____ 5. The primary goal of the _____ is for children to "learn how to learn."

_____ 6. Child care centers sponsored by _____ help reduce the conflict between home and work.

_____ 7. _____ is an example of a publicly sponsored program.

_____ 8. A large percentage of parents choose child care programs based on the advice of _____.

_____ 9. The emphasis of _____ care is on keeping the environment safe and healthy for young children.

_____ 10. _____ child care programs are funded by governments, school districts, or social service agencies.

_____ 11. Some kindergartens focus more on _____ development than on preacademic skills.

_____ 12. The largest group of privately sponsored programs is the _____.

_____ 13. The most common type of child care in the United States is _____.

_____ 14. Fees charged at a _____ are often less than at other programs.

_____ 15. _____ is stressed in Montessori schools.

Types of Programs

Name _____

Date _____ Period _____

Listed below are sentences describing the types of early childhood programs. Read each sentence and write the letter of the type of program it best describes. Letters will be used more than once.

_____ 1. Dental, medical, and mental health services are provided for children.

_____ 2. Interaction between the child and materials is highly structured.

_____ 3. Licensing rules for this type of child care are difficult to enforce.

_____ 4. Provide a place for child care while parents or guardians are at work or school.

_____ 5. Stress the theory that children learn best by being active.

_____ 6. Stress vocational education for future child care professionals.

_____ 7. Exist to provide training for future teachers and to serve as a study group for research.

_____ 8. Allow secondary students to work with the preschool children of high school students, faculty, and community members.

_____ 9. Are part of many school systems today and require children to be at least five years old.

_____ 10. Enrolled children spend about half the day in creative activities.

_____ 11. Developed to meet the developmental needs of children from low-income homes.

_____ 12. Five- to ten-year-old children most often attend.

_____ 13. The teacher may experience a lack of control.

_____ 14. Most common type of child care in the United States.

_____ 15. Usually open early in the morning and stay open until early evening.

_____ 16. Formed and run by parents who wish to take part in their children's preschool experiences.

_____ 17. Provide care before or after school hours.

_____ 18. Provide nutritious meals for many children who do not receive well-balanced meals at home.

_____ 19. The teacher's role is more passive than in other programs.

_____ 20. Child care is provided in a private home.

_____ 21. Parents make the administrative decisions.

_____ 22. Are located on postsecondary or college campuses.

A. child care centers

B. family child care

C. Head Start programs

D. kindergartens

E. laboratory schools

F. school-age child care

G. Montessori schools

H. parent cooperatives

I. high school child care programs

Choosing a Program

Name _____

Date _____ Period_____

Read each of the following situations and choose the type of early childhood program that you feel would be best. Explain why you chose each program.

1. Mary had a baby six weeks ago. She promised her employer that she would return to work. Now she needs to make child care arrangements. She prefers to have her child cared for with only two or three other children. What type of care is Mary looking for?

2. Sung Lee and Lia both work eight hours a day. Total travel time to and from work takes another hour and a half. They are seeking child care in a group setting within a few miles of their home. What kind of program would be best for Sung Lee and Lia?

(Continued)

3. Joyce is a single, unemployed mother. She has twin three-year-olds who are having speech problems. What type of program would meet Joyce's needs for her children?

4. Larry and Marge want their daughter, Lori, to become independent. They also want a program that stresses academic learning. What type of program would meet Larry and Marge's needs?

5. Phil and Maria have a seven-year-old daughter, Elisa. They need care for Elisa from four to six o'clock each evening. In what type of program might Elisa participate?

Evaluating Early Childhood Programs

Activity D

Chapter 2

Name _____

Date _____ Period _____

Pretend you are a parent looking for an early childhood program for your child. Visit two centers and evaluate them by checking the appropriate answers to the questions listed below. Then summarize your overall impressions of each program. Tell which one you would choose for your child and why.

Name of center #1: _____

Name of center #2: _____

Questions to Ask	Center #1		Center #2	
	Yes	No	Yes	No
1. Do the children appear to be happy, active, and secure?				
2. Are all staff members trained in early childhood education?				
3. Do staff members attend in-service training, professional meetings, and conferences on a regular basis?				
4. Are staff meetings conducted regularly to plan and evaluate program activities?				
5. Do staff members observe, assess, and record each child's developmental progress?				
6. Is the indoor and outdoor environment large enough to support a variety of activities?				
7. Is there equipment provided to meet all four areas of development: social, emotional, cognitive, and physical?				
8. Are safe and sanitary conditions maintained within the building and on the play yard?				
9. Are teacher-child interactions positive?				
10. Do teachers prepare daily and weekly lesson plans?				
11. Are parents welcome to observe and participate?				
12. Is sufficient equipment available for the number of children attending?				
13. Does the climate in the center "feel" positive?				
14. Do staff meet with parents on a regular basis to discuss the child's needs, interests, and abilities?				
15. Is the center accredited by the National Academy of Early Childhood Programs?				

(Continued)

Name _____

Overall impressions of center #1: _____

_____

_____

_____

_____

_____

Overall impressions of center #2: _____

_____

_____

_____

_____

_____

Which center would you choose and why?_____

_____

_____

_____

_____

_____

Observing Children: A Tool for Assessment

3

Check Your Understanding

Activity A

Chapter 3

Name _____

Date _____ Period _____

Read the following statements related to assessment. Circle *T* if the statement is true or *F* if the statement is false.

T F 1. Observation is one of the newest methods of learning about children.

T F 2. Assessment is the process of observing, recording, and documenting children's growth and behavior.

T F 3. Evaluation is the process of reviewing the information and finding value in it.

T F 4. Assessment keeps the teacher and curriculum responsive to the needs of children.

T F 5. A child's strengths and weaknesses can be identified through the assessment process.

T F 6. A single assessment is an exact assessment of ability or performance.

T F 7. Formal assessment is often used by early childhood teachers.

T F 8. Developmental norms are characteristic behaviors considered normal for children in specific age groups.

T F 9. Teachers prefer to use only one method for gathering information about the children.

T F 10. Anecdotal records are the simplest form of direct observation.

T F 11. Anecdotal records should include generalizations about the motives, attitudes, and feelings of the children.

T F 12. Observations should always be factual and unbiased.

T F 13. An anecdotal record requires no special setting or time frame.

T F 14. An interpretation attempts to explain observed behavior and give it meaning.

T F 15. Interpretations may be influenced by feelings, values, and attitudes.

T F 16. Checklists may be developed to survey one child or a group of children.

T F 17. Using a participation chart, teachers sometimes find children's activity preferences do not match their needs.

T F 18. Rating scales require you to make a judgment about behavior.

T F 19. A child's random scribbles on paper are not needed for assessment purposes.

T F 20. A portfolio can show the child's growth and development over time.

Assessment Tools Summary

Name _____

Date _____ Period _____

For each of the assessment tools listed, give possible advantages and disadvantages to their use. Then give an instance when this tool could effectively be used. Use your text to complete the chart as much as possible. Use other references or give your own opinion in order to complete the remaining portions of this chart.

Anecdotal Records		
Advantages:	Disadvantages:	Use:

Checklists		
Advantages:	Disadvantages:	Use:

(Continued)

Participation Chart		
Advantages:	Disadvantages:	Use:

Rating Scale		
Advantages:	Disadvantages:	Use:

Interpreting the Data

Name _____

Date _____ Period_____

Read the incident recorded on the anecdotal record shown in Figure 3-6 of your text. Then try your hand at interpreting the data by answering the questions below. Compare your interpretation with a classmate's and answer the remaining questions.

Your interpretation:

1. Why did Carrie hit and push Tony?_____

_____

2. What might have been her motive? _____

_____

3. Could someone or something have caused Carrie to act this way? _____

_____

4. Why did Carrie smile as Tony left?_____

_____

5. Why did Tony respond as he did when he was hit and shoved?_____

_____

6. What might have been his motive for shrugging and walking away? _____

_____

7. Could someone or something have caused Tony to act this way? _____

_____

Comparing interpretations:

Since no two people interpret facts in the same way, read the interpretation of this incident written by one of your classmates.

1. How did your classmate's interpretation differ from yours?_____

_____

_____

_____

2. What explanation can you give for this difference? _____

_____

_____

_____

3. What conclusions can you draw from this comparison?_____

_____

_____

_____

Designing an Assessment Tool

Activity D

Chapter 3

Name _____

Date _____ Period_____

Teachers often create their own assessment tools to meet their specific classroom needs. Design a simple checklist, participation chart, or rating scale in the space provided below. Use the developmental traits information in the Appendix of your text to make your chart or scale. Also refer to the samples in your text. Add lines as needed to your chart to design your assessment tool.

Type of assessment tool being designed: _____

Age of child for which it is designed:_____

Category of skill(s) being assessed (fine motor, gross motor, self-help skills, etc.): _____

_____

Category of Skills Being Assessed:	
Skills, Tasks, or Activities	

Copyright Goodheart-Willcox Co., Inc.

Observing Children: A Tool for Assessment   23

Understanding Children from Birth to Age Two

Types of Development

Name _____

Date _____ Period_____

Read each of the following skills and behaviors. Then place a check in the column that identifies the type of development being illustrated by each skill or behavior.

	Physical Development	Cognitive Development	Social-Emotional Development
1. Recognizes the voice of a parent.			
2. Gives "just two" on request.			
3. Answers routine questions.			
4. Understands *smaller*.			
5. Rides a tricycle.			
6. Smiles at a familiar face.			
7. Can point to body parts.			
8. Understands the pronoun *we*.			
9. Creeps.			
10. Does not like to share toys.			
11. Counts to five.			
12. Points to a circle.			
13. Understands *same size*.			
14. Marches to music.			
15. Says no just to see what will happen.			
16. Tells original stories.			
17. Hurls a ball.			
18. Follows a three-step command.			
19. Is patient and generous.			
20. Jumps in place.			

Reflexes

Name _____

Date _____ Period_____

Write a brief statement describing the behavior exhibited with each of the reflexes listed below.

1. Rooting: _____

_____

_____

_____

_____

2. Moro: _____

_____

_____

_____

_____

3. Palmar grasp: _____

_____

_____

_____

_____

4. Babinski: _____

_____

_____

_____

_____

5. Stepping or walking: _____

_____

_____

_____

_____

Understanding Development

Activity C

Activity C

Chapter 4

Name _____

Date _____ Period_____

Complete the following sentences by writing the correct words in the blanks.

attachment	cognitive	reflex
deferred imitation	motor sequence	separation anxiety
fine motor	object permanence	social-emotional
gross motor	physical	temperament
infant	preschooler	toddler

_____ 1. A(n) _____ is an automatic body response to a stimulus.

_____ 2. A child is called a(n) _____ during the first year after birth.

_____ 3. The understanding that objects exist even if you cannot see them is known as _____.

_____ 4. When a child is unhappy because a caregiver is leaving, the child is showing _____.

_____ 5. Children demonstrate _____ by watching another person's behavior and acting it out later.

_____ 6. _____ development involves the improvement of skills using large muscles.

_____ 7. _____ behaviors show that infants care for and respond to certain people who are important to them.

_____ 8. _____ development involves learning to relate to others and refining feelings and expressions of feelings.

_____ 9. The way a child reacts to his or her environment reflects the child's _____.

_____ 10. _____ development refers to changes in the body.

_____ 11. The term _____ refers to the order in which a child is able to perform new movements.

_____ 12. The term which describes a child who is between the ages of three and six years is _____.

_____ 13. _____ development involves skills which relate to the small muscles.

_____ 14. From the first year until the third birthday, a child is called a(n) _____.

_____ 15. _____ development refers to the mental processes used to gain knowledge.

Encouraging Development

Activity D

Chapter 4

Name _____

Date _____ Period_____

Talk with an early childhood teacher to learn about activities, equipment, objects, and teaching approaches he or she uses to encourage development in children from birth to two years of age. Seek information related to each area of development listed. Record your findings below and share them with the class.

Physical development:

_____

_____

_____

_____

_____

_____

_____

_____

Cognitive development:

_____

_____

_____

_____

_____

_____

_____

_____

_____

_____

Social-emotional development:

_____

_____

_____

_____

_____

_____

_____

_____

_____

Understanding Two- and Three-Year-Olds

Development of Two-Year-Olds

Activity A

Chapter 5

Name _____

Date _____ Period _____

Use the information in the text to answer the following questions about two-year-olds.

1. What advances in the area of gross motor development are usually observed in two-year-olds? _____
   _____
   _____
   _____

2. What advances in the area of fine motor development are usually observed in two-year-olds? _____
   _____
   _____
   _____

3. Explain the difference between comprehension skills and expressive language skills. Which skills do
   children develop sooner? _____
   _____
   _____
   _____

4. What math readiness skills do two-year-olds have? _____
   _____
   _____
   _____

5. What types of experiences do two-year-olds enjoy acting out as they play? _____
   _____
   _____

6. How do most two-year-olds feel about possessions and what actions display this attitude? _____
   _____

(Continued)

7. Why are fears so common among two-year-olds? _____

_____

_____

8. How can a teacher encourage a two-year-old's emotional development? _____

_____

_____

9. List at least four important considerations for teachers of two-year-olds.

_____

_____

_____

Studying Two-Year-Olds

Activity B

Chapter 5

Name _____

Date _____ Period_____

Interview one or both parents of a two-year-old child. Ask how that child has developed and changed in the past year in relation to each of the areas listed. If necessary, explain each type of development to the parent or parents you are interviewing. Then compare the child's actual development with the usual development for two-year-olds as described in the text.

Gross motor development	Fine motor development
Self-help skills	**Language comprehension**
Expressive language skills	**Math readiness**
Social development	**Emotional development**

What usual developments of two-year-olds has this child not yet achieved?_____

_____

_____

_____

_____

In what ways has this child matured beyond the level of most two-year-olds? _____

_____

_____

_____

_____

Development of Three-Year-Olds

Activity C

Chapter 5

Name _____

Date _____ Period _____

Use the text to answer the following questions about three-year-olds.

1. What new gross motor skills do three-year-olds have?_____
   _____
   _____

2. List some new fine motor skills of three-year-olds. _____
   _____
   _____
   _____
   _____

3. In what way are the thinking skills of the three-year-old more mature than the thinking skills of the two-year-old?
   _____
   _____

4. What flaws still exist in the three-year-old's ability to think? _____
   _____
   _____

5. What new language comprehension skills do three-year-olds develop?_____
   _____
   _____
   _____
   _____

6. What new expressive language skills do three-year-olds develop?_____
   _____
   _____
   _____

7. What new math readiness developments can be observed in three-year-olds?_____
   _____
   _____
   _____

8. How does a three-year-old's attitude toward possessions differ from a two-year-old's attitude toward
   possessions?_____
   _____
   _____
   _____

(Continued)

9. How do three-year-olds handle their emotions? _____

_____

_____

_____

10. How do three-year-olds usually express their anger? _____

_____

_____

11. What are four important considerations when teaching three-year-olds? _____

_____

_____

_____

_____

Studying Three-Year-Olds

Name _____

Date _____ Period_____

Interview one or both parents of a three-year-old child. Ask how that child has developed and changed in the past year in relation to each of the areas listed. Refer to the text to explain the types of development to the parent or parents you are interviewing. Then compare the child's actual development with the usual development for three-year-olds described in the text.

Gross motor development	Fine motor development
Self-help skills	Language comprehension
Expressive language skills	Math readiness
Social development	Emotional development

What usual developments of three-year-olds has this child not yet achieved? _____

_____

_____

_____

_____

In what ways has this child matured beyond the level of most three-year-olds?_____

_____

_____

_____

_____

Self-Help Skills

Activity E

Chapter 5

Name _____

Date _____ Period _____

Read the following list of self-help skills. Write two **(2)** beside each skill that is usually mastered by a two-year-old and three **(3)** beside each skill that is usually mastered by a three-year-old.

_____ 1. Opens snaps and zippers.

_____ 2. Gets through the night without wetting.

_____ 3. Works buckles.

_____ 4. Puts on shoes that do not tie.

_____ 5. Begins to cooperate in dressing.

_____ 6. Pours liquid from a small pitcher.

_____ 7. Removes socks, shoes, and pants.

_____ 8. Washes and dries face and hands.

_____ 9. Closes snaps.

_____ 10. Uses knife for spreading.

_____ 11. Pulls on simple garments.

_____ 12. Starts using the toilet when reminded.

_____ 13. Turns faucet on and off.

_____ 14. Has almost full control over toilet routines.

_____ 15. Unbuttons large buttons.

_____ 16. Seldom has bowel accidents.

Language Skills

Name _____

Date _____ Period_____

Read the following list of language skills. Determine whether each is a language comprehension skill or an expressive language skill. Place a *C* in front of skills that are language comprehension. Place an *E* in front of skills that are expressive language skills.

_____ 1. Combines two or more words such as "Boy hit."

_____ 2. Understands and answers routine questions such as "What is your name?"

_____ 3. Uses prepositions in speech.

_____ 4. Follows three-part instruction.

_____ 5. Points to six body parts on self or doll.

_____ 6. Uses three-word sentences such as "You go home."

_____ 7. Says "I want more cookies."

_____ 8. Uses negative terms such as "Mommy don't go."

_____ 9. Gives "just two" on request.

_____ 10. Understands the pronouns *you* and *they.*

_____ 11. Uses possessives such as "Mommy's coat."

_____ 12. Understands *smaller.*

_____ 13. Understands *larger.*

_____ 14. Provides appropriate answers for *how* questions.

_____ 15. Joins two sentences with a conjunction.

Understanding Four- and Five-Year-Olds

The Truth About Preschoolers

Activity A

Chapter 6

Name _____

Date _____ Period _____

Read the following statements. Circle *T* if the statement is true or *F* if the statement is false.

T F 1. Four- and five-year-olds usually express their anger by hitting other children.

T F 2. Verbal jokes are easy to understand for most four-year-olds.

T F 3. Some preschoolers begin losing their baby teeth.

T F 4. In a passive voice sentence, the subject of the sentence is placed before the object.

T F 5. Imaginary playmates are normal among four- and five-year-olds.

T F 6. Most four-year-olds understand that a dime is worth more than a nickel.

T F 7. Articulation is the ability to speak in clearly pronounced sounds.

T F 8. Four- and five-year-olds draw objects exactly the way they see them.

T F 9. At five and one-half years, children have legs that are about one-third the length of their bodies.

T F 10. Children learn to use irregular verbs during this preschool stage.

T F 11. Asking a child to be a helper builds self-esteem.

T F 12. Four- and five-year-olds do not fully understand what is and is not dangerous.

T F 13. Few four- and five-year-olds can walk on a balance beam.

T F 14. Most four- and five-year-olds are able to read.

T F 15. At age five, children use words related to ideas or thought in their daily language.

T F 16. Four- and five-year-olds prefer to have friends of the same sex.

T F 17. True counting usually comes before rote counting.

T F 18. Preschool children tend to talk to you rather than have a conversation with you.

T F 19. Four- and five-year-olds are not yet able to understand passive voice sentences.

T F 20. The writing and drawing skills of four- and five-year-olds improve quickly.

T F 21. Preschoolers tend to take literally statements that have more than one meaning.

T F 22. Asking questions is a way children try to make sense of their world.

T F 23. Stuttering usually results when a preschooler talks faster than he or she can think.

T F 24. Rote counting is reciting numbers in their proper order.

T F 25. Four- and five-year-olds may become reckless in working to improve their physical skills.

T F 26. Five-year-olds have a vocabulary of about 2000 words.

T F 27. By four years of age, most children use a fork to cut large pieces of food.

Reading and Math Fun

Name _____

Date _____ Period_____

Using people or written materials as references, locate one rhyme, song, or game that could be used to develop reading skills and one rhyme, song, or game that could be used to develop math skills. Write the rhyme, song, or a description of the game in the space provided. Then tell what specific skills the activity will promote. Demonstrate both activities for the class.

Reading Activity

Skills this activity will promote: _____

_____

_____

_____

_____

_____

(Continued)

Name _____

Math Activity

Skills this activity will promote: _____

_____

_____

_____

_____

_____

Handling Emotions

Activity C

Chapter 6

Name _____

Date _____ Period _____

Read a current magazine article on helping preschoolers cope with such emotions as fear, anger, jealousy, or sadness. Summarize the article in the space provided. Present your report orally to the class.

Article Title: _____

Author: _____

Source: _____

Summary: _____

_____

_____

_____

_____

_____

_____

_____

_____

_____

_____

_____

_____

_____

_____

_____

_____

_____

_____

_____

_____

_____

_____

_____

_____

_____

_____

_____

_____

_____

_____

_____

Developing Activities

Activity D　　　　　　　　Name _____

Chapter 6　　　　　　　　　Date _____ Period_____

Think of one original activity a teacher could use to help four- and five-year-olds in each area of development listed below. Describe the activities in the space provided and share them with others in the class.

Gross motor development: _____

_____

_____

_____

_____

_____

_____

_____

_____

Fine motor development:_____

_____

_____

_____

_____

_____

_____

_____

_____

Language comprehension:_____

_____

_____

_____

_____

_____

_____

_____

_____

(Continued)

Name _____

Expressive language: _____
_____
_____
_____
_____
_____
_____
_____

Math skills: _____
_____
_____
_____
_____
_____
_____
_____
_____
_____

Social development: _____
_____
_____
_____
_____
_____
_____
_____

Emotional development: _____
_____
_____
_____
_____
_____
_____
_____
_____

Understanding Middle Childhood Terms

Activity A

Chapter 7

Name _____

Date _____ Period_____

Match the following terms and definitions by placing the correct letters in the corresponding blanks.

_____ 1. Span of years between age 6 and 12.

_____ 2. Ability to see objects in a distance more easily than those that are close by.

_____ 3. Ability to see close objects more clearly than those at a distance.

_____ 4. Using logic but basing it on what has been seen or experienced.

_____ 5. Excessive body fat.

_____ 6. Technique children often use to remember information.

_____ 7. Manipulation of ideas based on logic rather than perception.

_____ 8. Ability to arrange items in increasing or decreasing order based on volume, size, or weight.

_____ 9. Change in position or shape of substances does not change the quantity.

_____ 10. Ability to group items by common attributes.

_____ 11. Process where people define themselves in terms of qualities, skills, and attributes they see in others.

_____ 12. Belief that you are a worthwhile person.

_____ 13. Ability to understand the feelings of others.

_____ 14. Being aware of others' distress and wanting to help them.

_____ 15. Understanding and using accepted rules of conduct when interacting with others.

_____ 16. The process of acquiring the standards of behavior considered acceptable by society.

A. moral development

B. farsighted

C. operation

D. classification

E. self-esteem

F. middle childhood

G. obesity

H. rehearsal

I. social comparison

J. empathy

K. nearsighted

L. seriation

M. conservation

N. morality

O. compassion

P . concrete operations

Check Your Gender IQ

Name _____

Date _____ Period_____

The text describes many differences in physical development and social behavior between boys and girls during the school-age years. Read the following statements. In the blank before each statement, write **G** if the statement generally describes girls and **B** if the statement generally describes boys. Then try to observe school-age children during a school recess period and answer the questions at the end of this activity.

_____ 1. Taller at the beginning of this stage.

_____ 2. Tend to occupy space closer to the school building.

_____ 3. Are more open than secretive in their relationships.

_____ 4. Interact in pairs or small groups.

_____ 5. Best at skills requiring balance, flexibility, or rhythm.

_____ 6. Reach 80 percent of adult height by the end of middle childhood.

_____ 7. Play involves more taking turns and cooperating with others.

_____ 8. Experience a growth spurt at age 12.

_____ 9. Have more physical strength.

_____ 10. Prefer jumping rope and doing tricks on the jungle gym.

_____ 11. Tend to control large fixed spaces at school that are used for team sports.

_____ 12. Weigh more by 12 years of age.

_____ 13. Experience a growth spurt at age 10.

_____ 14. Prefer competitive sports.

Observe a large group of school-age children of the same age during a school recess period. Look for the gender differences listed above. Then answer the questions below.

1. Which of the above characteristics about boys were you able to observe?

_____

_____

_____

2. Which of the above characteristics about girls were you able to observe?

_____

_____

_____

3. It is important that early childhood teachers do not reinforce gender-role stereotypes. However, gender differences do exist among school-age children. How do you feel a teacher should respond to this dilemma?

_____

_____

_____

_____

Health Dilemmas

Name _____

Date _____ Period _____

The situations below describe challenges you might face in handling health-related situations in the classroom. Break into small groups. Read each dilemma and discuss possible approaches to the situations. Write your group's best suggestions in the spaces provided.

1. You notice that Antwann, a seven year old, holds books four or five inches in front of his face. What might be his problem? What action should you take?

_____

_____

_____

_____

_____

_____

_____

_____

_____

2. Toby's behavior is frustrating you. He seems to ignore most suggestions. After listening to a story, his responses to questions are inaccurate. What action should you take?

_____

_____

_____

_____

_____

_____

_____

3. Rhonda is an obese child. At lunch and during snack time, she takes more food than needed. As her teacher, what can you do to help Rhonda with her weight problem? How would you suggest working with Rhonda's parents?

_____

_____

_____

_____

_____

_____

Testing Mental Operations

Activity D

Chapter 7

Name _____

Date _____ Period _____

Children learn the concepts of conservation, seriation, and classification during the middle years. Design your own activities to test these concepts with a child between the ages of six and ten. After testing the child, record their responses below.

Age of child tested: _____

Conservation

Describe how you plan to test the child's understanding of the concept of conservation:

_____

_____

_____

What supplies will you need? _____

_____

What results do you expect that will show that the child understands conservation? _____

_____

_____

What were the results of your test with the child? _____

_____

_____

Seriation

Describe how you plan to test the child's understanding of the concept of seriation: _____

_____

_____

What supplies will you need? _____

_____

What results do you expect that will show that the child understands seriation? _____

_____

_____

What were the results of your test with the child? _____

_____

_____

(Continued)

Classification

Describe how you plan to test the child's understanding of the concept of classification: _____

_____

_____

_____

What supplies will you need? _____

_____

What results do you expect that will show the child understands classification? _____

_____

_____

What were the results of your test with the child? _____

_____

_____

_____

_____

_____

Beliefs About Middle Childhood

Name _____

Date _____ Period_____

Read each sentence and circle the word choice that best describes your beliefs. Then explain your answer in the space provided.

1. I believe friendships take on a **lesser/greater** importance in middle childhood than before.

    Reason: _____

    _____

    _____

    _____

2. I believe teachers **can/cannot** play an important role in building a school-age child's self-esteem.

    Reason: _____

    _____

    _____

    _____

3. I believe children **should be/should not be** encouraged to participate in team sports and competition during middle childhood.

    Reason: _____

    _____

    _____

    _____

4. I believe playing games that involve rules **is/is not** important to a school-age child's development.

    Reason: _____

    _____

    _____

    _____

Preparing the Environment 8

Meeting the Goals of a Well-Planned Space

Activity A   Name _____

Chapter 8   Date _____ Period_____

Pretend that you have been hired as the director of a new child care center. You have been asked to provide input into the design of the physical space. For each of the goals for a well-planned space listed below, give two examples of how you would meet that goal in designing the physical space.

Goal 1: To provide a physically safe environment for the children.

_____

_____

_____

Goal 2: To provide children with areas that promote cognitive, emotional, social, and physical growth.

_____

_____

_____

Goal 3: To provide adults with a space that is easy to supervise.

_____

_____

_____

Goal 4: To provide space that is pleasing to the eye for both adults and children.

_____

_____

_____

Goal 5: To provide easy access to materials when needed so children are able to direct themselves.

_____

_____

_____

Goal 6: To encourage children to take part in activities.

_____

_____

Responses to Color

Name _____

Date _____ Period_____

Match the colors in the right column with the appropriate psychological response in the left column.

Psychological Response   **Color**

_____   1. Clean and cool.   A. light blue

_____   2. Comfortable, soothing, and secure.   B. light green

_____   3. Calm, refreshing, peaceful, and restful.   C. orange

_____   4. Happy and cheerful.   D. purple

_____   5. Welcoming, forceful, and energetic.   E. red

_____   6. Stimulating.   F. white

_____   7. Mournful.   G. yellow

8. Which colors can be used to make a room appear larger?

_____

_____

_____

9. Which colors tend to make a room appear smaller?

_____

_____

_____

10. List three factors to consider when selecting a color for the classroom.

_____

_____

_____

_____

_____

_____

Activity Areas

Name _____

Date _____ Period_____

List ten basic activity areas found in most classrooms. Name their functions and describe where each should be placed in the classroom.

1. _____
   _____
   _____
   _____

2. _____
   _____
   _____
   _____

3. _____
   _____
   _____
   _____

4. _____
   _____
   _____
   _____

5. _____
   _____
   _____

6. _____
   _____
   _____
   _____

7. _____
   _____
   _____

8. _____
   _____
   _____

(Continued)

9. _____
   _____
   _____
   _____

10. _____
    _____
    _____
    _____

Planning the outdoor play area is just as important as planning the indoor classroom areas. Answer the following questions about outdoor play areas.

11. List three guidelines for the best use of play yard space.

    _____
    _____
    _____
    _____

12. What are nine other items to consider when planning an outdoor play yard?

    _____
    _____
    _____
    _____
    _____
    _____
    _____
    _____

Selecting Toys, Equipment, and Educational Materials

9

Toys Meeting Goals

Activity A

Chapter 9

Name _____

Date _____ Period_____

Listed below are two program goals for a group of three-year-olds. Read the goals and available toys and equipment. Then list additional toys and equipment that are needed to help meet the program goals.

Program Goals	Available Toys and Equipment	Toys and Equipment Needed
Goal A: To encourage language development.	*Books*	
Goal B: To encourage fine motor development.	*Puzzles*	

Think of two or more possible program goals for a group of three-year-olds. List the program goals and toys that could help meet those goals.

Program Goals	Toys and Equipment Needed
Goal A:	
Goal B:	

Age Appropriate Equipment

Name _____

Date _____ Period _____

Not all toys and equipment are appropriate for children of all ages. While some toys are suitable for infants, other toys are only appropriate for older children. Match the toys and equipment listed below with the age of the youngest children who should use them. Refer to Chart 9-8 in the text if necessary.

_____ 1. Activity gym.

_____ 2. Roller skates.

_____ 3. Cloth books.

_____ 4. Wooden telephone.

_____ 5. Tricycle.

_____ 6. Doll bed.

_____ 7. Play dough.

_____ 8. Small jungle gym.

_____ 9. Blunt scissors.

_____ 10. Pull toys.

_____ 11. Large wooden threading beads.

_____ 12. Giant dominoes.

_____ 13. Hard books.

_____ 14. Stacking and nesting toys.

_____ 15. Blunt scissors.

_____ 16. Walking board.

_____ 17. Scooter.

_____ 18. Coaster wagon.

_____ 19. Doll carriage.

_____ 20. Simple climber and slide.

A. six-month to one-year-old

B. one-year-old

C. two-year-old

D. three-year-old

E. four-year-old

F. five-year-old

Actions to Take

Activity C

Chapter 9

Name _____

Date _____ Period_____

List an action you could take to improve the safety and performance of the toys and equipment listed below. Some items may need to be discarded.

Condition or Toy to Improve	Action to Take
1. Chipped paint.	
2. Worn varnish.	
3. Loose nuts.	
4. Rusty equipment.	
5. Squeaky bicycle wheels.	
6. Broken plastic toy.	
7. Play iron with cord and plug.	
8. Toy gun.	

(Continued)

Condition or Toy to Improve	Action to Take
9. War game.	
10. Pull toy with small beads inside.	
11. Swing seat with open S-ring.	
12. Stuffed animal with button eyes.	
13. Balloons.	
14. Wooden swing seat.	
15. Exposed screws and bolts.	

Comparing Prices

Name _____

Date _____ Period_____

Find the price charged for each of the following items by three different sources. For instance, check prices in catalogs, stores, and co-ops. You might also try to check prices of secondhand equipment. Record each price and the source of your information in the space provided. Also record any other notes you want to remember about that source.

Easel

Vendor 1:	Vendor 2:	Vendor 3:
_____	_____	_____
Price (including any shipping costs:)	Price (including any shipping costs:)	Price (including any shipping costs:)
_____	_____	_____
Other important notes:	Other important notes:	Other important notes:
_____	_____	_____
_____	_____	_____

Sensory Table

Vendor 1:	Vendor 2:	Vendor 3:
_____	_____	_____
Price (including any shipping costs:)	Price (including any shipping costs:)	Price (including any shipping costs:)
_____	_____	_____
Other important notes:	Other important notes:	Other important notes:
_____	_____	_____
_____	_____	_____

Tricycle

Vendor 1:	Vendor 2:	Vendor 3:
_____	_____	_____
Price (including any shipping costs:)	Price (including any shipping costs:)	Price (including any shipping costs:)
_____	_____	_____
Other important notes:	Other important notes:	Other important notes:
_____	_____	_____
_____	_____	_____

(Continued)

Bookshelf

Vendor 1:	Vendor 2:	Vendor 3:
_____	_____	_____
Price (including any shipping costs:)	Price (including any shipping costs:)	Price (including any shipping costs:)
_____	_____	_____
Other important notes:	Other important notes:	Other important notes:
_____	_____	_____
_____	_____	_____

Autoharp®

Vendor 1:	Vendor 2:	Vendor 3:
_____	_____	_____
Price (including any shipping costs:)	Price (including any shipping costs:)	Price (including any shipping costs:)
_____	_____	_____
Other important notes:	Other important notes:	Other important notes:
_____	_____	_____
_____	_____	_____

12 Cans Tempera Paint

Vendor 1:	Vendor 2:	Vendor 3:
_____	_____	_____
Price (including any shipping costs:)	Price (including any shipping costs:)	Price (including any shipping costs:)
_____	_____	_____
Other important notes:	Other important notes:	Other important notes:
_____	_____	_____
_____	_____	_____

Talk to people at two centers to learn whether the price quotations you received were realistic and whether a center could afford to pay those prices. Also ask for tips on how to obtain necessary equipment at the lowest possible cost. Record what you learn from these discussions.

_____

_____

_____

Promoting Children's Safety  10

Safety Procedures

Activity A

Name _____

Chapter 10

Date _____ **Period**_____

Choose terms from the following list to correctly fill in the blanks in the statements related to safety.

child abuse	fire drills	physical	self-control
dangers	fire extinguishers	protection education	spills
electrical	food	rules	walk
environment	glass	seat belts	windows
evacuation			

_____ 1. Constantly be alert to potential _____, or unsafe situations.

_____ 2. The staff is responsible for planning a safe _____ for the children.

_____ 3. Planning safety _____ will help you meet the safety goal.

_____ 4. Post _____ procedures to use in various emergencies.

_____ 5. Immediately report suspected cases of _____ to the appropriate community agency.

_____ 6. Schedule an in-service on how to use _____ before the opening of the center.

_____ 7. Center vans and buses should have _____ in them to protect children.

_____ 8. Include _____ in the curriculum to teach children how to handle possible sexual advances from adults.

_____ 9. Child care centers are responsible for providing proper _____ storage.

_____ 10. Require staff to obtain an approved _____ exam before working with children.

_____ 11. Children who lack _____ and are hazardous to themselves and others should be removed from the classroom.

_____ 12. _____ outlets must be covered.

_____ 13. Remind children to _____ indoors rather than running.

_____ 14. Wipe up _____ right away.

_____ 15. Beware of stuffed toys that may have button or _____ eyes.

_____ 16. Schedule _____ on a regular basis such as once a month to practice evacuating the building.

_____ 17. Keep _____ closed at all times unless gates or sturdy screens are in place.

Fire Safety Evaluation

Name _____

Date _____ Period_____

Visit a child care center. Use the checklist below to evaluate fire safety practices at the center. Read each statement and place a check mark in the appropriate column. Then answer the following questions.

Fire Safety Checklist	Yes	No
1. Exit passageways and exits are free from furniture and equipment.		
2. Locks on bathroom doors and toilet stalls can be opened easily from the outside by center staff.		
3. Protective covers are on all electrical outlets.		
4. Permanent wiring is used instead of lengthy extension cords.		
5. Each wall outlet contains no more than two electrical appliances.		
6. A fire evacuation plan is posted.		
7. Fire drills are conducted monthly.		
8. Flammable, combustible, and other dangerous materials are marked and stored in areas accessible only to staff.		
9. Children are restricted to floors with grade level exits (no stairs).		
10. The basement door is kept closed.		
11. There is no storage under stairs.		
12. Fire extinguishers are in place and checked regularly.		
13. Smoke alarms and fire alarms are checked at least once a month.		
14. Matches are kept out of the reach of children.		
15. Toys, chairs, tables, and other equipment are made of flame-retardant materials.		
16. Carpets and rugs are treated with a flame-retardant material.		

                                                 Poor   Good   Excellent

1. How would you rate this center's fire safety practices?   1   2   3   4   5

2. Explain your answer. _____

_____

_____

3. Would you add any additional items to the checklist above? Why or why not? _____

_____

_____

4. Why do you think it is important to find and correct fire safety hazards in a child care center?_____

_____

_____

Understanding Child Abuse

Name _____

Date _____ Period _____

Using the information in the text, other reference materials, and your own opinions, respond to the following:

1. List and describe the four types of child abuse. _____

   _____

   _____

   _____

   _____

   _____

   _____

   _____

   _____

   _____

   _____

   _____

   _____

2. Research an agency that helps prevent child abuse and/or works with people in child abuse situations. What support services are offered for families, and how are child abuse situations handled? How is a child abuse case reported? Record what you learn. _____

   _____

   _____

   _____

   _____

   _____

   _____

   _____

   _____

   _____

   _____

   _____

   _____

   _____

   _____

   _____

   _____

   _____

(Continued)

3. List and describe several characteristics that many child abusers have in common. _____

_____

_____

_____

_____

_____

_____

_____

_____

_____

_____

_____

4. What current social problems do you think contribute to today's problem of child abuse?

_____

_____

_____

_____

_____

_____

_____

_____

_____

_____

_____

5. What do you think teachers can do to help protect children from child abuse? _____

_____

_____

_____

_____

_____

_____

_____

_____

_____

_____

Planning Nutritious Meals and Snacks

Nutrients and Their Functions

Activity A

Chapter 11

Name _____

Date _____ Period_____

Match the following terms and identifying phrases.

_____ 1. Build and repair tissues.

_____ 2. Carries fat-soluble vitamins.

_____ 3. Helps prevent night blindness.

_____ 4. Is a part of hemoglobin.

_____ 5. Helps cells use other nutrients.

_____ 6. Aids in blood clotting.

_____ 7. Helps promote normal appetite and digestion.

_____ 8. Helps build bones and teeth.

_____ 9. Helps carry waste products from cells.

_____ 10. Helps regulate many body processes.

_____ 11. Provide bulk in the form of cellulose (needed for good digestion).

_____ 12. Helps keep skin, tongue, and lips healthy.

_____ 13. Helps body fight infection.

_____ 14. Acts as antioxidant.

_____ 15. Helps keep adult bones healthy.

A. calcium

B. carbohydrates

C. fat

D. iron

E. niacin

F. phosphorus

G. proteins

H. riboflavin

I. thiamin

J. vitamin A

K. vitamin C

L. vitamin D

M. vitamin E

N. vitamin K

O. water

Nutrition Crossword

Name _____

Date _____ Period_____

[Crossword grid]

Across

2. The most important nutrient provided by the milk group is _____.
5. A child's serving may be about _____ the size of an adult's serving.
7. Deep yellow and dark green vegetables are rich sources of _____.
8. The most important nutrient supplied by the meat group is _____.
9. The science of food and how the body uses it is called _____.
11. Many milk products have been _____ to include vitamins A and D.
12. _____ is a condition that can lead to health problems such as hypertension in diabetes during adulthood.
13. The main sources of the mineral _____ are meat and meat alternates.
14. Chemical substances needed for growth and maintenance of health and found in foods are called _____.

Down

1. A child's diet should include six servings from the _____ group daily.
3. Not eating enough food to keep a healthy body weight and activity level is called _____.
4. _____ is a lack of nutrients in the diet.
6. Using the _____ for Young Children is an easy way to plan a nutritious diet.
7. Citrus fruits are rich sources of _____.
10. Taking in more food than the body needs to function properly is called _____.

Food Guide Pyramid for Young Children

Name _____

Date _____ Period _____

A variety of food items are listed below. Place each of these items under the correct food group in the Food Guide Pyramid for Young Children.

cottage cheese	apples	cheese	pea pods
collard greens	waffles	meatballs	crackers
kidney beans	granola	peanut butter	yogurt
chow mein noodles	broccoli	cheese fondue	dates

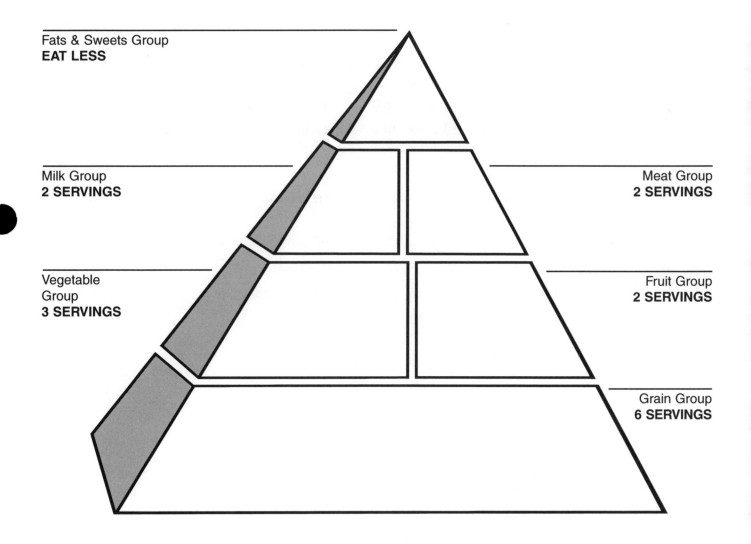

Fats & Sweets Group
EAT LESS

Milk Group
2 SERVINGS

Meat Group
2 SERVINGS

Vegetable
Group
3 SERVINGS

Fruit Group
2 SERVINGS

Grain Group
6 SERVINGS

Identifying the Sources

Name _____

Date _____ Period_____

For each group of sources listed, fill in the blank with the name of the nutrient provided. Use each nutrient listed only once.

Carbohydrates	Fats	Niacin
Proteins	Riboflavin	Thiamin
Vitamin A	Vitamin C	Vitamin D
Vitamin E	Vitamin K	

_____ 1. Egg yolk, organ meats, cauliflower, and leafy green vegetables.

_____ 2. Peanut butter, lentils, meat, poultry, fish, eggs, and dairy products.

_____ 3. Milk, cheese, ice cream, yogurt, liver, meat, fish, poultry, and dark green leafy vegetables.

_____ 4. Breads, cereals, corn, peas, beans, potatoes, pasta, fruits, vegetables, honey, sugar, jam, jelly, molasses.

_____ 5. Butter, cheese, cream, nuts, olives, chocolate, bacon, and salad oil.

_____ 6. Dark green and yellow fruits and vegetables, whole milk, butter, cream, fortified margarine, and cheeses.

_____ 7. Whole grain cereals, liver, eggs, fats, and green vegetables.

_____ 8. Brewer's yeast, enriched or whole grain breads and cereals, dried beans, pork, and fish.

_____ 9. Sunshine, tuna, sardines, fish liver oils, liver, butter, and fortified milk.

_____ 10. Tomatoes, cantaloupe, broccoli, and citrus fruits.

_____ 11. Dried beans, peas, whole grain cereals, fish, milk, poultry, and meat.

Guiding Children's Health 12

Health Match

Activity A

Chapter 12

Name _____

Date _____ Period _____

Match the following terms and definitions.

_____ 1. An injury caused by heat, radiation, or chemical agents.

_____ 2. A break in the skin.

_____ 3. A disease that results from a virus, breaks down the immune system, and, over time, can be fatal.

_____ 4. A scrape that damages a portion of the skin.

_____ 5. Condition in which a person has periodic seizures.

_____ 6. A disease caused by a viral infection of the nervous system and brain and commonly spread through animal bites.

_____ 7. Damage to the surface of the skin or body tissue.

_____ 8. Illnesses that can be passed to other people.

_____ 9. Small bugs that live on the hair and scalp and lay eggs called nits.

_____ 10. Can occur as a result of an extremely allergic reaction.

_____ 11. A reaction of the body to a substance in the environment.

_____ 12. An injury to the tissue directly under the skin's surface.

_____ 13. Disease in which the body cannot properly control the level of sugar in the blood.

_____ 14. A hormone needed to keep sugar in the blood at a proper level.

_____ 15. An illness caused by eating food that contains harmful bacteria, toxins, parasites, or viruses.

_____ 16. Virus that breaks down the immune system and, over time, can lead to a more advanced disease.

_____ 17. A course of action that controls future decisions.

A. abrasion

B. policy

C. burn

D. closed wound

E. communicable diseases

F. diabetes

G. epilepsy

H. foodborne illness

I. allergy

J. head lice

K. insulin

L. open wound

M. HIV

N. anaphylactic shock

O. rabies

P. wound

Q. AIDS

Communicable Diseases

Name _____

Date _____ Period_____

List the symptoms and incubation periods for the communicable diseases listed below. Refer to pages 179 to 180 in the text.

Disease	Symptoms	Incubation Period
Chicken pox		
Conjunctivitis		
Hepatitis A		
Haemophilus influenzae type B		
Mumps		
Lice		
Ringworm		
Rubella		
Scabies		
Streptococcal infections		

First Aid Kit Scramble

Activity C

Chapter 12

Name _____

Date _____ Period_____

Unscramble the letters below to reveal items that belong in a child care center's first aid kit. Write the name of each item in the blank that follows it.

1. rstfi dia naanulm _____

2. elirste srift ida ssdsergni _____

3. rtsewzee _____

4. tunlb dppeit sssrocis _____

5. yfeats sinp _____

6. eic cakp _____

7. aasegnbd zeagu _____

8. isevehad etap _____

9. ttheeemmorr _____

10. aatintcbreila nisk rclenea _____

11. ypusr fo ccaepi _____

12. aamenilc oontil _____

13. rosabbtne ttoonc llsab _____

14. oohllca peiws _____

15. dmli opas _____

16. eevisadh aaebndgs _____

17. elbasopsid reppa ssseuti _____

18. tfgsialhhl _____

Burns

Match the following descriptions to the types of burns described by placing the correct letter in the corresponding blank. Letters will be used more than once.

_____　　1.　The least severe burns.

_____　　2.　Destroy nerve endings in the skin.

_____　　3.　Require immediate medical attention.

_____　　4.　Common signs include mild discoloration or redness.

_____　　5.　Can quickly become third-degree burns if infection arises.

_____　　6.　An ambulance should be called immediately.

_____　　7.　Healing is normally rapid.

_____　　8.　Are likely to swell a great deal over a period of several days.

_____　　9.　May result from brief contact with hot objects.

_____　10.　Only the top layer of skin is damaged.

A.　first-degree burns

B.　second-degree burns

C.　third-degree burns

11.　Describe how you should treat a first-degree burn. _____

_____

_____

_____

_____

12.　Describe what you would and would not do if a child suffered a second-degree burn. _____

_____

_____

_____

_____

13.　What would you do if a child received a third-degree burn? _____

_____

_____

_____

_____

Developing Guidance Skills

Direct and Indirect Guidance

Activity A　　　　　　　　　Name _____

Chapter 13　　　　　　　　　Date _____ Period _____

Read each of the following statements and decide whether *direct* or *indirect* guidance is being described. Record your responses on the blank provided.

_____ 1. Removing a hot kettle from the cooking area.

_____ 2. Offering a child choices.

_____ 3. Telling a child what to do.

_____ 4. Lowering the easel so the children can comfortably reach the paper.

_____ 5. Moving a child's coat hook to a lower position in his or her locker.

_____ 6. Saying to a child, "Mary, you need to pick up that paper."

_____ 7. Telling Tom, "You'll lose your turn if you keep pushing."

_____ 8. Adding simple puzzles to the small manipulative area.

_____ 9. Providing a place mat with an outline of a glass, plate, spoon, and fork.

_____ 10. Suggesting to Wendy that she place her arm around Kris, who is crying.

_____ 11. Telling a child that her painting is beautiful.

_____ 12. Keeping your back to the wall so you can observe the entire classroom.

_____ 13. Reminding children to cover their mouths when they cough.

_____ 14. Placing a picture of the toy wagon on the shelf where it is stored.

_____ 15. Purchasing two additional scooters for the play yard since the scooter is a popular choice during free play.

_____ 16. Encouraging the children to work together by saying, "Ask Eve if she can help you."

_____ 17. Recognizing a child's accomplishment by saying, "I like the way you helped Amy."

_____ 18. Providing training scissors in the art area so Amanda can learn to cut.

_____ 19. Showing approval by smiling at Jamal after he finished a puzzle.

_____ 20. Seating Ethan and Chris apart during story time to prevent arguments.

Positive Guidance

Name _____

Date _____ Period _____

Children are more likely to respond to positive statements than negative ones. Rewrite each statement below so it tells the child what he or she is expected to do.

1. "Don't put the scissors on the floor." _____

   _____

2. "Quit yelling." _____

   _____

3. "Don't spill your milk." _____

   _____

4. "Don't walk in front of the slide." _____

   _____

5. "You'll get water on your clothes." _____

   _____

6. "Don't spill sand." _____

   _____

7. "You're pouring too fast." _____

   _____

8. "Don't get the book dirty." _____

   _____

9. "Don't walk so slow." _____

   _____

10. "Don't touch all the muffins." _____

    _____

11. "Don't ride on the grass." _____

    _____

12. "You're hurting the bunny." _____

    _____

13. "Get off the gym." _____

    _____

14. "Don't eat the macaroni with your fingers." _____

    _____

Putting Effective Guidance into Practice

Activity C

Chapter 13

Name _____

Date _____ Period _____

For each of the guidance techniques listed below, describe a situation where it would be appropriate to use. Then describe what you would do and say in each situation. Include all dialogue.

Positive Reinforcement

Describe the situation. _____

_____

_____

Describe how you would use positive reinforcement. _____

_____

_____

Natural Consequences

Describe the situation. _____

_____

_____

Describe how you would use natural consequences. _____

_____

_____

Artificial Consequences

Describe the situation. _____

_____

_____

Describe how you would use artificial consequences. _____

_____

_____

I-Message

Describe the situation. _____

_____

_____

Describe how you would use an I-message. _____

_____

_____

Promoting a Positive Self-Concept

Describe the situation. _____

_____

_____

Describe how you would use this situation to promote the child's self-concept. _____

_____

_____

Guidance Techniques

Activity D

Chapter 13

Name _____

Date _____ Period_____

Match each of the following statements to the letter of the guidance technique it illustrates. Then write an example of your own for each guidance technique listed.

_____ 1. "Sharon, paint only on your own paper. If you paint on Sandra's paper again, you'll have to move."

_____ 2. "Sally, let's draw on the chalkboard instead."

_____ 3. "Sue, what are the rules for using the jungle gym?"

_____ 4. "I liked the way you helped Kelsie."

_____ 5. "Wendy is having a temper tantrum. Pay no attention to her."

_____ 6. "Tommy, here is a paper towel."

_____ 7. "Peggy, I'm sorry. Here is a glass of juice."

_____ 8. "Lucia, I know you can do it!"

_____ 9. John said, "Steve won't give me play dough." The teacher repeated the statement. Then she added, "You're angry because Steve will not give you play dough."

_____ 10. "Use this pair of scissors. It does not have glue on its cutting edge, so it will cut easier."

A. ignoring

B. active listening

C. modeling

D. persuading

E. praising

F. prompting

G. encouraging

H. redirecting

I. suggesting

J. warning

1. _____
   _____

2. _____
   _____

3. _____
   _____

4. _____
   _____

5. _____
   _____

6. _____
   _____

7. _____
   _____

8. _____
   _____

9. _____
   _____

10. _____
    _____

Guidance Problems  14

Guidance Match

Activity A

Chapter 14

Name _____

Date _____ Period _____

Match the terms in the right column with their descriptions in the left column.

_____ 1. A form of body language used by very young children who cannot express themselves using words.

_____ 2. Engaging in this activity in public is considered improper.

_____ 3. This tension-relieving behavior usually peaks at 18 months.

_____ 4. Many children experience this emotion on the first day of school.

_____ 5. Used by insecure children as a way of getting attention.

_____ 6. The larger the group, the greater the likelihood this state of overexcitement will occur.

_____ 7. An external factor that affects each child differently.

_____ 8. When children feel they are not in control, they may have these feelings of discouragement.

_____ 9. Feelings of tensions that can be caused by both negative and positive events.

_____ 10. Is common between two and three years of age as children attempt more independence.

A. biting

B. exploring the body

C. fear

D. frustration

E. negativism

F. noise

G. overstimulation

H. stress

I. thumbsucking

J. tattling

Choose one of the causes or reactions to tension listed above. Describe an instance where you observed this behavior in a young child. Explain how the adult (or you) handled the situation.

_____

_____

_____

_____

_____

_____

_____

_____

_____

_____

_____

Guidance Tips

Name _____

Date _____ Period _____

Read the following statements related to guiding children. Circle *T* if the statement is true or *F* if the statement is false.

T F   1. To avoid problems caused by noise, controlling the volume of tapes, records, and CDs works well.

T F   2. Increasing the volume of your voice will cause children's voices to become softer.

T F   3. Preparing materials in advance can cut down on waiting time.

T F   4. Providing several kinds of toys allows children to choose the activities that reflect their needs and interests.

T F   5. When you notice a child is under stress, its good to remain close to the child and comfort him or her.

T F   6. If children steal, it is best to lecture them.

T F   7. On certain occasions, young children should be allowed to hit each other.

T F   8. Aggression can be relieved by yelling, beating drums, dancing to loud music, crying, and making animal noises.

T F   9. Children who bite should be bitten back.

T F 10. It is better to ignore thumbsucking than to pressure children to stop.

T F 11. Children often need to act out situations to conquer their fears.

T F 12. When children are afraid, they sometimes hit.

T F 13. Children need to be alerted to changes in activities or routines well in advance.

T F 14. It may be necessary to speed children along so the class activities remain on schedule.

T F 15. You should suggest that an aggressive child sit down and look at a book.

T F 16. A positive event, such as a new pet, can cause stress.

T F 17. A sudden change in a child's behavior can be a bad sign of stress.

T F 18. Instead of ignoring tattling behavior, you should speak to the child who has broken the rule.

T F 19. Overstimulation, changes in routine, and loud noises can cause tension in young children.

T F 20. Overstimulation is more common with a small group of children than with a large group.

T F 21. Children usually demonstrate positive behavior when asked to wait for a long time.

T F 22. The most common age for negativism is between four and five years.

T F 23. To prevent tattling, you should work to build the child's self-esteem.

T F 24. Children may reject a person or situation that feels strange or unsafe.

Analyzing Behavior

Name _____

Date _____ Period_____

Many factors must be considered in guiding children. Some of these factors are listed below. All the vowels in the key words are missing. Supply the missing vowels and tell why each factor deserves consideration.

1. ___ g ___ should be considered when guiding children because _____
   _____
   _____
   _____

2. C ___ ___ s ___ s of tension must be understood when guiding young children because _____
   _____
   _____
   _____

3. ___ v ___ rst ___ m ___ l ___ t ___ ___ n should be considered when guiding young children because
   _____
   _____
   _____

4. M ___ t ___ r ___ ___ ls and equipment should be considered when guiding young children because
   _____
   _____
   _____

5. Ph ___ s ___ c ___ l problems must be considered when guiding young children because _____
   _____
   _____
   _____

6. Str ___ ss should be considered when guiding young children because _____
   _____
   _____
   _____

Dialing for Answers

Name _____

Date _____ Period_____

In the following exercise, the numbers below the blanks represent letters on the telephone dial. Use the clues and numbers to complete the following statements relating to guidance problems.

1	**ABC** **2**	**DEF** **3**
GHI **4**	**JKL** **5**	**MNO** **6**
PRS **7**	**TUV** **8**	**WXY** **9**
*	**0**	**#**

1. Guidance problems often occur in the form of __ __ __ __ __ __ __ __ __ __ behavior.
                           3 4 7 7 8 7 8 4 8 3

2. __ __ __ __ __ __ __ __ __ __ __ can create tensions and cause children to feel they are not in control.
   3 7 8 7 8 7 2 8 4 6 6

3. Behavior can be affected by poor or inadequate __ __ __ __ __ __ __ __ __.
                          6 8 8 7 4 8 4 6 6

4. One cause of __ __ __ __ __ __ __ for children is the breakup of a family.
           7 8 7 3 7 7

5. To help reduce stress, promote a __ __ __ __ __ __ __ __ __ environment.
               7 6 7 4 8 4 8 3

6. Between two and three years of age, preschool children can be __ __ __ __ __ __ __ __.
                     6 3 4 2 8 4 8 3

7. The greatest number of __ __ __ __ __ __ __ __ __ usually occurs at about 18 months of age.
           8 2 6 8 7 8 6 7

8. Young children should never be allowed to __ __ __ other children.
            4 4 8

9. It is not unusual behavior for a two-year-old to __ __ __ __.
           2 4 8 3

10. __ __ __ __ __ __ __ __ __ __ __ is a tension-relieving behavior.
   8 4 8 6 2 7 8 2 5 4 6 4

Establishing Classroom Rules

Stating the Positive

Activity A Name _____

Chapter 15 Date _____ Period_____

Rules should be stated in a language the children can understand. They should also be simple, short, and positive. Rules should always give the children direction. State the following rules positively, telling the children what to do.

Example rule	Rule rewritten in positive form
1. Don't stand on the slide.	
2. Don't leave the spills.	
3. Don't leave the puzzle on the floor.	
4. Don't tear the pages of the book.	
5. Don't run in the classroom.	

Rule Pyramid

Name _____

Date _____ Period _____

Fill the pyramid with the words that are missing from the statements.

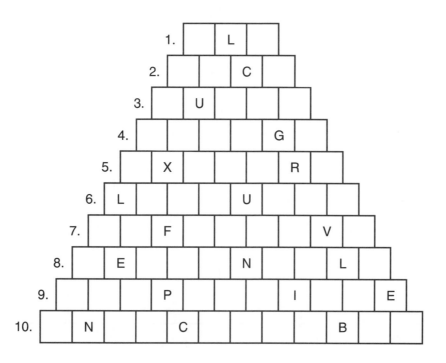

1. _____ employees should have a copy of classroom rules.

2. When a child is _____, the child may need more time to meet the demands of the teacher.

3. Every area of the classroom needs to have _____.

4. Any _____ in rules should always be discussed with the staff.

5. Children feel freer to _____ when they know their teacher will stop them if they go too far.

6. Rules should be written in a _____ children understand.

7. _____ rules serve as a kind of shorthand that state the goals of the center.

8. Rules that are not _____ can cause young children to feel angry.

9. Teachers are _____ for suggesting new rules to the director and staff.

10. _____ behavior needs to be stopped.

Know the Rules

Activity C

Chapter 15

Name _____

Date _____ Period _____

Circle *T* if the statement is true or *F* if the statement is false.

T F 1. Rules are necessary only on the playground.

T F 2. The director's responsibility is to consistently maintain classroom rules.

T F 3. A copy of the rules should be posted on the bulletin board in the teacher's lounge and/or in the classroom.

T F 4. Rules help children develop self-control.

T F 5. Rules should be stated negatively, in terms of behavior to avoid.

T F 6. Unreasonable rules can cause young children to feel angry.

T F 7. All rules should have a useful function.

T F 8. Rules need to be re-examined on a regular basis by the entire staff.

T F 9. When a rule no longer fits the group's needs, it should be discarded.

T F 10. Unacceptable behavior should be stopped firmly and quickly.

T F 11. Rules need to be inflexible.

T F 12. Depending upon the material being used for sensory play, rules may change somewhat.

T F 13. Children must wash their hands before participating in a cooking activity.

T F 14. Rules in the art area are usually minimal.

T F 15. Teachers need to demonstrate some of the rules in the science area.

Describe what you think might happen if a center did not have rules. _____

_____

_____

_____

_____

_____

_____

_____

_____

_____

_____

_____

Setting Rules

Name _____

Date _____ Period _____

Each of the areas in a center needs rules. Think of eight rules that a center might have in addition to the rules discussed in the text and list them in the space provided. Indicate the area of the center to which each rule relates.

1. _____
   _____

2. _____
   _____

3. _____
   _____

4. _____
   _____

5. _____
   _____

6. _____
   _____

7. _____
   _____

8. _____
   _____

Visit a center and list five of their most important rules.

1. _____
   _____

2. _____
   _____

3. _____
   _____

4. _____
   _____

5. _____
   _____

How do the rules of the center compare with your rules and the rules discussed in the text? _____
_____
_____
_____
_____

Handling Daily Routines

Your Style of Managing Daily Routines

Activity A

Chapter 16

Name _____

Date _____ Period_____

Indicate whether you agree or disagree with the following statements about daily routines. Explain your answers in the space provided.

Agree Disagree

_____ _____ 1. Children benefit from following a daily schedule.

_____

_____

_____

_____ _____ 2. Children gain satisfaction by doing things for themselves.

_____

_____

_____

_____ _____ 3. Teachers should always assist children.

_____

_____

_____

_____ _____ 4. Teachers should plan an activity during the arrival time to make the separation from parents easier.

_____

_____

_____

_____ _____ 5. Children should be responsible for hanging up their own coats.

_____

_____

_____

_____ _____ 6. Demonstrating at the child's eye level is the most effective.

_____

_____

_____

(Continued)

Agree Disagree

_____ _____ 7. Children should be required to tie their own shoes by age three.

_____
_____
_____

_____ _____ 8. All children must nap.

_____
_____
_____

_____ _____ 9. Four-year-old children should assist in setting the lunch table.

_____
_____
_____

_____ _____ 10. Children should be reprimanded when they spill milk.

_____
_____
_____

_____ _____ 11. Children should be served only one tablespoon of food for each year of age.

_____
_____
_____

_____ _____ 12. Snacks should be provided between meals for children who refuse to eat breakfast.

_____
_____
_____

_____ _____ 13. A dawdling child should be threatened.

_____
_____
_____

_____ _____ 14. Repeated vomiting should be ignored if you are sure the child is not ill.

_____
_____
_____

_____ _____ 15. Toilet learning should be required of children attending a preschool program.

_____
_____
_____

Planning a Daily Schedule

Activity B

Chapter 16

Name _____

Date _____ Period_____

Working in a small group, plan a daily schedule for a child care center. Complete the form below as you develop your plans.

Group members: _____

Name of your child care center: _____

Age group and type of program you are offering (all-day, half-day, two-hour): _____

_____

General goals of your program: _____

_____

Fill in the schedule below, giving times, activities, procedures, and rationale for each time segment.

Daily Schedule			
Time	**Activity**	**Procedures**	**Rationale**

Managing Conflicts

Name _____

Date _____ Period_____

Read each of the following situations. Then work in small groups to discuss them. Write a suggestion for solving each of the conflicts in a positive way.

1. Four-year-old Shyrell refuses to take off her coat. When she arrived at school, she went directly to the art area, picked up a paintbrush, and began to paint. How could you handle this situation?

   _____

   _____

   _____

   _____

2. Toby had a birthday last week. He is now four years old. He still depends on the teacher to help him put on his outdoor clothing. Will this cause Toby to become more dependent or more independent? What advice do you have for the teacher?

   _____

   _____

   _____

   _____

3. Sally does not appear to have an interest in food. Every day her teacher reminds her to eat during mealtime. Sally does not seem to take the teacher's advice. Sometimes the teacher even tries to feed Sally, but this does not appear to be effective. What advice do you have for Sally's teacher?

   _____

   _____

   _____

   _____

4. All children are expected to remain at the table until everyone is finished eating. However, Christine usually leaves the table before her peers have finished. So far her teacher has been ignoring this behavior. How may Christine's behavior affect the other children? What actions should Christine's teacher take?

   _____

   _____

   _____

   _____

5. After lying down on their cots at nap time, Rivka and Kato ask for a drink of water. This happens every day. Many times after they get water, the other children also request it. How can you prevent this from happening?

   _____

   _____

   _____

   _____

Dog Flowchart

Activity A

Chapter 17

Name _____

Date _____ Period_____

Review the section on flowcharts in the text. Create a flowchart listing the possible concepts to be used in developing a theme on dogs. Then write objectives related to this theme.

Dogs

Objectives:

1. _____

2. _____

3. _____

4. _____

5. _____

6. _____

Learning Activities Related to a Theme on Dogs

Activity B

Chapter 17

Name _____

Date _____ Period _____

List below activities that you could use under each curriculum area for a theme focusing on dogs.

Art:

Storytelling:

Sensory Table:

Dramatic Play:

Music:

Science:

Math:

Fingerplays:

Behaviors

Name _____

Date _____ Period_____

Check all the behaviors below that could be used in a lesson plan.

_____ 1. weigh	_____ 15. lace	_____ 29. really understand
_____ 2. ask	_____ 16. color	_____ 30. name
_____ 3. catch	_____ 17. clap	_____ 31. throw
_____ 4. paint	_____ 18. think	_____ 32. tie
_____ 5. follow	_____ 19. taste	_____ 33. believe
_____ 6. know	_____ 20. roll	_____ 34. wipe off
_____ 7. climb	_____ 21. say	_____ 35. write
_____ 8. cut	_____ 22. collect	_____ 36. fully appreciate
_____ 9. remove	_____ 23. understand	_____ 37. locate
_____ 10. believe	_____ 24. turn	_____ 38. nail
_____ 11. feed	_____ 25. sit	_____ 39. tap
_____ 12. mark	_____ 26. appreciate	_____ 40. recognize
_____ 13. button	_____ 27. touch	
_____ 14. enjoy	_____ 28. stand	

Select six of the behaviors you checked and use them to write learning objectives. Be sure your objectives include all three parts: the conditions of performance, the behavior, and the level of performance.

1. _____
   _____

2. _____
   _____

3. _____
   _____

4. _____
   _____

5. _____
   _____

6. _____
   _____

Curriculum Building

Activity D

Chapter 17

Name _____

Date _____ Period _____

Fill in the squares with the correct terms.

The vertical highlighted column spells: **CURRICULUM BUILDING**

1.								A	N	D				C			—												
2.														U															
3.														R															
4.														R															
5.														I															
6.														C															
7.														U															
8.														L															
9.														U															
10.														M															
11.														B															
12.														U															
13.														I															
14.														L		—													
15.														D	—														
16.														I															
17.														N															
18.														G															

1. Approach to learning where learning is seen as a constant process of exploring and questioning.

2. Children who learn best through hearing.

3. Objectives that list what tools the child will use.

4. Objective that states the minimum standard of achievement.

5. Statements that describe the expected outcomes of an activity.

6. Overall view of the curriculum which outlines general plans.

7. Based on the concept that as children grow, their circle of interests becomes larger.

8. Outlines specific actions and activities that will be used to meet program goals.

9. Children who depend a great deal on sense of sight for learning.

10. Broad statements of purpose that reflect the end result of education.

11. Any visible activities done by the child.

12. How an activity will end.

13. Movement from one activity to another.

14. Children who prefer working alone and are often the first to try something new.

15. Children who like to work with others in groups and like to follow models when learning new activities.

16. How you will gain the children's attention.

17. Activities planned with a specific goal in mind.

A Sample Lesson

Activity E

Chapter 17

Name _____

Date _____ Period _____

Write a sample lesson plan for a group activity of your choice. Fill in the information requested in the space provided and share your plan with others in class.

Date: _____ Time: _____

Group: _____

Activity: _____

Goals: _____

_____

_____

_____

_____

_____

_____

_____

Learning objectives: _____

_____

_____

_____

_____

_____

Materials needed: _____

_____

_____

_____

_____

Motivation/introduction: _____

_____

_____

_____

_____

_____

(Continued)

Name _____

Procedures: _____

_____

_____

_____

_____

_____

_____

_____

Closure/transition: _____

_____

_____

_____

_____

Evaluation: _____

_____

_____

_____

_____

_____

Guiding Art, Blockbuilding, and Sensory Experiences

Stages of Artwork

Activity A

Chapter 18

Name _____

Date _____ Period _____

Match the following stages of art skill development with their description.

_____ 1. Occur between 15 months and 3 years of age.

_____ 2. Child attempts to mimic own view of the world.

_____ 3. Occur when the child is between three and four years of age.

_____ 4. Crudely drawn human figures are common.

_____ 5. Children do not make the connection between the marks on the paper and their own movements.

_____ 6. Occur during the fourth and fifth year.

_____ 7. Children learn basic forms such as ovals, rectangles, and circles.

_____ 8. First stage of artwork.

_____ 9. Children create symbols of people or objects they know.

_____ 10. Children are first able to control the size and shape of a line.

_____ 11. Children may begin to name their drawings.

_____ 12. Children produce their first real drawing.

_____ 13. The resulting art is merely a byproduct of the experience.

_____ 14. Cars, boats, and airplanes may appear in children's artwork.

_____ 15. Children first see the connection between their own movements and the marks they make on the page.

A. scribbles

B. basic forms

C. first drawings

Characteristics of Children's Art

Name _____

Date _____ Period _____

Duplicate a child's artwork for each of the three stages listed. Indicate the appropriate ages for each stage and describe characteristics of the artwork.

Scribbles	**Age:** **Characteristics of art:**
Basic Forms	**Age:** **Characteristics of art:**
First Drawings	**Age:** **Characteristics of art:**

Sources of Free Art Materials

Activity C

Chapter 18

Name _____

Date _____ Period_____

Brainstorm a list of free materials that could be obtained from each of the following sources. Try to include at least five items that could be obtained from each source.

Bakery	Doctor's office
_____	_____
_____	_____
_____	_____
_____	_____
_____	_____

Bank	Eye doctor
_____	_____
_____	_____
_____	_____
_____	_____
_____	_____

Bookstore	Fabric store
_____	_____
_____	_____
_____	_____
_____	_____
_____	_____

Dentist	Florist
_____	_____
_____	_____
_____	_____
_____	_____
_____	_____

Grocery store	Newspaper/printer
_____	_____
_____	_____
_____	_____
_____	_____
_____	_____

(Continued)

Name _____

Hair stylist	Paint store
_____	_____
_____	_____
_____	_____
_____	_____
_____	_____
Jewelry store	**Shoe store**
_____	_____
_____	_____
_____	_____
_____	_____

Tips for Buying Art Supplies

Pretend you are a director purchasing art supplies for your center. Next to each of the following items, indicate with a check mark whether you would purchase the item or acquire it through donations. If you plan to have the item donated, list possible sources in the community.

Art Supplies	Purchase	Donate	Sources of Donations
Newsprint			
Wallpaper			
Fabric			
Plastic foam			
Packing materials			
Magazine pictures			
Buttons			
Cardboard			
Egg cartons			
Paper plates			
Chalk and crayons			
Scissors			
Glue and paste			

Rating Play Dough

Name _____

Date _____ Period_____

Prepare the three play dough recipes included in the text: refrigerator play dough, sawdust play dough, and cooked play dough. Rank them according to the criteria listed. Use a scale of 1 to 3 with 1 being the best rating. Total the scores for each play dough. The play dough with the lowest rating has the best score.

	Stickiness	Softness	Odor	Texture	Visual Appeal	Keeping Quality	Total Score
Refrigerator Play Dough General Reaction:							
Sawdust Play Dough General Reaction:							
Cooked Play Dough General Reaction:							

Which play dough would you prefer to use in the classroom and why?

_____

_____

_____

_____

_____

Storytelling

Activity A

Chapter 19

Name _____

Date _____ Period_____

Read the following statements about storytelling. Circle *T* if the statement is true or *F* if the statement is false.

T   F   1.   Book reviews provide descriptions of books to avoid.

T   F   2.   Children can develop a love for stories and books as a result of daily storytelling experiences.

T   F   3.   Most preschool children can separate fact from fiction.

T   F   4.   Storytelling is a way to present information.

T   F   5.   Three-year-olds are usually ready for fantasy stories.

T   F   6.   It is important to have highly detailed illustrations for children.

T   F   7.   Social understanding is the theme of family life stories.

T   F   8.   Two-year-olds remain interested in a book for five to eight minutes.

T   F   9.   Three-year-olds are interested in books that contain many sentences on each page.

T   F   10.   Four-year-olds appreciate humor in books.

T   F   11.   *Little Red Riding Hood* would be an excellent book for a group of three- and four-year-olds.

T   F   12.   Oral reading skills can be developed by practicing in front of a mirror.

T   F   13.   You can set the mood for a story by making a personal comment.

T   F   14.   Whispering or shouting can add interest to a story.

T   F   15.   If children do not appear to like a story, talking faster may help.

T   F   16.   Speaking too slowly when storytelling is a common problem.

T   F   17.   A clear ending to a story is not necessary if children are paying attention.

T   F   18.   Draw-and-tell stories may be prepared so they can be used more than once.

T   F   19.   If you lack drawing skills, you should not use flipcharts.

T   F   20.   Keeping books and art supplies in the same area is a good way to conserve space.

Choosing Books for Children

Name _____

Date _____ Period _____

Pretend you are writing a column for a parents' magazine. Next to each of the following ages, list tips for selecting books.

Children's Age	Tips for Selecting Books
Birth to two years of age	
Two years of age	
Three years of age	
Four years of age	
Five years of age	

Story Comparisons

Name _____

Date _____ Period _____

Select three books that a teacher might read to children in a certain age group and compare the books in the chart provided.

Age group selected: _____

	Book #1	Book #2	Book #3
Book title:			
Description of book:			
Props that could be used in telling story:			
Positive features of book:			
Negative features of book:			
Concluding comments:			

Evaluate Your Storytelling Technique

Name _____

Date _____ Period_____

Choose a partner. Select a book to read to a small group of children. Have your partner watch and evaluate you using the following checklist. Then evaluate your partner using the same checklist. Answer the questions that follow.

Excellent	Good	Needs Improvement	
_____	_____	_____	1. Chose a developmentally-appropriate book for the children.
_____	_____	_____	2. Used a good introduction to establish the mood of the story.
_____	_____	_____	3. Explained unfamiliar words.
_____	_____	_____	4. Encouraged child participation.
_____	_____	_____	5. Told the story with a conversational tone.
_____	_____	_____	6. Used eye contact.
_____	_____	_____	7. Conveyed enthusiasm.
_____	_____	_____	8. Demonstrated good posture.
_____	_____	_____	9. Used different voices for particular characters to create interest.
_____	_____	_____	10. Pronounced words clearly.
_____	_____	_____	11. Used a lively tempo.
_____	_____	_____	12. Allowed children to add comments to the story.
_____	_____	_____	13. Held the book in a way that allowed children to see the pictures.

What are your strengths?_____

_____

What are your weaknesses? _____

_____

What steps can you take to improve your skills? _____

_____

_____

_____

_____

Playtime Match

Activity A

Chapter 20

Name _____

Date _____ Period _____

Match the following terms and definitions by placing the correct letters in the corresponding blanks.

_____ 1. Commenting to children who follow desired behavior.

_____ 2. Contains materials and equipment that encourages children to explore roles.

_____ 3. Form of social play in which several children play together as they imitate others.

_____ 4. The third stage of material use in play that occurs when children do not need realistic props to play.

_____ 5. Play between two or more children.

_____ 6. Children play by themselves, but stay close to other children.

_____ 7. Occurs when the teacher shows the correct behavior for children during their socio-dramatic play.

_____ 8. Form of play in which a child imitates others.

_____ 9. Giving human traits to nonliving objects.

_____ 10. Two or more forces that oppose each other.

_____ 11. Skill that requires the teacher to provide children with ideas for difficult situations.

_____ 12. Type of play that allows a child to imitate others while using puppets in play.

_____ 13. The second stage of material use that occurs when children use props as intended while playing with other children.

_____ 14. Form of play in which children play alone without involving other children.

_____ 15. Occurs when a child displaces his or her emotions onto an object.

_____ 16. Type of play in which children mimic various adult roles.

_____ 17. The first stage of material use which occurs when children handle the props they are given.

_____ 18. Figure designed in likeness to an animal or human.

A. prop box

B. coaching

C. conflict

D. cooperative play

E. dramatic play

F. reinforcing

G. functional stage

H. imaginative stage

I. manipulative stage

J. modeling

K. parallel play

L. personification

M. projection

N. puppet

O. puppetry

P. role-playing

Q. socio-dramatic play

R. solitary play

Encouraging Socio-Dramatic Play

Name _____

Date _____ Period _____

Prop boxes are used to extend children's play. In the space below, list materials that could be included in a prop box for an office worker, painter, baker, and carpenter. Think of two other categories and list the materials that could be included in a prop box for each of those categories.

Office Worker	Painter
Baker	**Carpenter**

Describe several actions a teacher could take to encourage children to participate in socio-dramatic play.

_____

_____

_____

_____

_____

_____

_____

_____

_____

_____

_____

Design a Puppet

Name _____

Date _____ Period_____

Design a puppet for use with preschool children. Answer the questions below.

1. What type of puppet are you designing? (hand, mascot, "me") _____

2. What is your puppet's name? _____

3. Sketch your design for the puppet:

4. List the materials you will need to create the puppet:

   _____   _____

   _____   _____

   _____   _____

   _____   _____

   _____   _____

   _____   _____

5. In what area of the curriculum could this puppet be used? _____
   Give specific examples for its use: _____

   _____

   _____

(Continued)

6. How could your puppet be used to learn more about what an individual child is thinking or feeling?_____

_____

_____

_____

7. Optional: If you are able to use your puppet with preschoolers, tell about your experience. How did you use the puppet? How did the children react to your puppet? _____

_____

_____

_____

_____

_____

_____

_____

_____

_____

Writing Puppet Stories

Activity D

Chapter 20

Name _____

Date _____ Period _____

Reread the information on puppets in the chapter. Then write a puppet story. Begin with a theme and develop a plot. Use the space below to write the story.

Theme: _____

_____

_____

_____

Story: _____

_____

_____

_____

_____

_____

_____

_____

_____

_____

_____

_____

_____

_____

_____

_____

_____

_____

_____

_____

_____

_____

_____

Name _____

Guiding Manuscript Writing Experiences  **21**

Practice Your Writing

Activity A

Chapter 21

Name _____

Date _____ Period_____

Using Chart 21-4 for guidance, take out a separate sheet of paper and practice making the uppercase letters, lowercase letters, and numerals 1-9 using the proper techniques. When you are satisfied with your work, reproduce the chart on this page.

_____

_____

_____

_____

_____

Explain several problems that children may have in the early stages of writing. _____

_____

_____

_____

As a teacher, what might you do to help these children? _____

_____

_____

Manuscript Writing

Activity B

Chapter 21

Name _____

Date _____ Period _____

Read each description listed below and write the answer in the blank.

_____ 1. Another name for manuscript writing.

_____ 2. This type of coordination involves muscle control that allows the hand to do a task the way the eye sees it done.

_____ 3. This type of writing can be done more quickly than manuscript.

_____ 4. Writing requires use of the fingers and hands, which are these kinds of muscles.

_____ 5. A difficult task for many beginning writers.

_____ 6. Type of line that may occur when children write too slowly.

_____ 7. This type of writing may be caused by a pencil that is too fine or too hard.

_____ 8. Common problem in which children write letters backwards.

_____ 9. The percentage of children who are left-handed.

_____ 10. Technique to use when a child is having difficulty writing a particular letter.

_____ 11. Letters that are half the size of capital letters in manuscript writing.

_____ 12. Another name for capital letters.

13. What materials can teachers display to encourage printing? _____

_____

_____

14. Name an activity you can use to help develop children's fine motor coordination. _____

_____

_____

15. Name an activity you can use to help develop children's hand-eye coordination. _____

_____

_____

Guiding Math Experiences 22

Math Match

Activity A   Name _____

Chapter 22   Date _____ Period_____

Match the following math terms with their definitions.

_____ 1. Groups of objects that are alike in some way and therefore belong together.

_____ 2. Process of physically separating objects into categories based on unique features.

_____ 3. A set with no members.

_____ 4. Method of assessment that involves giving children set activities to determine skills and/or needs.

_____ 5. Process of mentally grouping objects or ideas into categories based on some unique feature.

_____ 6. Involves attaching a number to a series of grouped objects.

_____ 7. Simple form of classification that allows children to join a new experience with a similar, earlier experience.

_____ 8. Form of classification that involves putting like objects together.

_____ 9. The recitation of numbers in order.

_____ 10. Blocks of varying colors and geometric shapes.

_____ 11. The understanding that one group has the same number as another.

_____ 12. Each of these number symbols represents a quantity.

A. classification

B. empty set

C. matching

D. numerals

E. one-to-one correspondence

F. parquetry blocks

G. rational counting

H. recognizing

I rote counting

J. sets

K. sorting

L. specific task assessment

Discussing Colors

Name _____

Date _____ Period_____

Read the name of each color listed. In the space provided, record your responses to each color. Then ask a preschool child to share his or her thoughts about each color. Record the child's responses. Answer the questions below the chart to note similarities and differences in the responses.

Color	My Thoughts	A Preschool Child's Thoughts
Red		
Blue		
Green		
Yellow		
Purple		
Pink		
Black		
Brown		

What similarities and differences did you find in the responses? _____

_____

_____

_____

_____

_____

What might be some reasons for the differences? _____

_____

_____

_____

_____

_____

Teaching Space, Size, Volume, and Time

Activity C

Chapter 22

Name _____

Date _____ Period_____

Space, size, volume, and time are four math concepts that are important for young children to learn. Specific terms related to each of these concepts are listed on this page. Think of an original way you could teach children to understand these terms and explain your method in the space provided.

Space Concepts

High and low: _____

_____

_____

_____

Here and there: _____

_____

_____

_____

Inside and outside:_____

_____

_____

_____

Top, center, and bottom: _____

_____

_____

Size Concepts

Big and little:_____

_____

_____

_____

Wide and thin: _____

_____

_____

_____

Inches and pounds: _____

_____

_____

_____

Smaller than and bigger than: _____

_____

_____

(Continued)

Volume Concepts

Much:_____

_____

_____

_____

Empty: _____

_____

_____

_____

Full: _____

_____

_____

_____

Some:_____

_____

_____

_____

Time Concepts

Day and night: _____

_____

_____

_____

Before and after: _____

_____

_____

_____

Now and later: _____

_____

_____

_____

New and old: _____

_____

_____

_____

Using Recipes to Teach Math Concepts

Name _____

Date _____ Period_____

Look through a cookbook and find two recipes that could be used for cooking activities to teach children math concepts. Record the recipes in the space provided and answer the questions.

Recipe: _____

What mathematical concepts and terms could this cooking activity teach children? _____

_____

_____

_____

_____

How could children participate in this activity? _____

_____

_____

_____

_____

(Continued)

Recipe: _____

What mathematical concepts and terms could this cooking activity teach children? _____

_____

_____

_____

_____

How could children participate in this activity? _____

_____

_____

_____

_____

Guiding Science Experiences  **23**

Science Overview

Activity A   Name _____

Chapter 23   Date _____ Period _____

Answer the following questions about science and science activities.

1. What is science? _____
   _____
   _____

2. What do children learn from using their senses to observe? _____
   _____
   _____
   _____

3. How can children benefit from studying science? _____
   _____
   _____
   _____
   _____
   _____

4. Why is the science area best located near the kitchen? _____
   _____
   _____

5. What factors should you consider when selecting equipment and materials for the science area? _____
   _____
   _____
   _____

6. List ten items you might find on a science table. _____
   _____
   _____
   _____
   _____
   _____

(Continued)

7. What are the five basic process skills that science activities should promote? _____

_____

_____

_____

_____

_____

8. Give an example of one way you can help children learn about each of the following senses.

   a. Feeling: _____

   _____

   _____

   b. Smelling: _____

   _____

   _____

   c. Seeing: _____

   _____

   _____

   d. Hearing: _____

   _____

   _____

   e. Tasting: _____

   _____

   _____

Forming Open-Ended Questions

Activity B

Chapter 23

Name _____

Date _____ Period_____

For each closed-ended question given, write a related open-ended question you could ask instead.

1. What happens to the ice when we add heat?

_____

2. Does a rabbit have fur?

_____

3. Does the potato stay hard inside when we cook it?

_____

4. Which object feels soft?

_____

5. Which classroom pet has fins for swimming?

_____

6. Does a bubble contain air?

_____

7. Does the magnet attract the plastic lids?

_____

8. Which item is a darker blue?

_____

9. To boil an egg, what must we put in the pot first?

_____

10. Who is the person in this picture?

_____

11. Does the tricycle have three wheels?

_____

12. Is soup warmer than pudding?

_____

13. How many legs does the canary have?

_____

14. Do magnets attract other magnets?

_____

15. Is the sandpaper scratchy or smooth?

_____ *(Continued)*

Pet Care

Name _____

Date _____ Period_____

Read the following statements about pets and the care they require. Circle *T* if the statement is true or *F* if the statement is false.

T F 1. Guinea pigs and rabbits eat similar foods.

T F 2. Rabbits actually eat very little.

T F 3. Guinea pigs need space in a cage to hide, exercise, and sleep.

T F 4. A rabbit's cage needs to be cleaned often.

T F 5. One strain of hamster spreads a form of meningitis.

T F 6. Rabbits should have wood for gnawing.

T F 7. Snakes should be placed in a wire rustproof cage.

T F 8. Hamsters enjoy lettuce, clover, alfalfa, and grass.

T F 9. Hamsters may bite when exposed to loud voices.

T F 10. Newspaper should be spread on the floor of a snake's aquarium.

T F 11. A pet shop salesperson or conservation authority worker can help you determine a snake's dietary needs.

T F 12. The larger species of snakes eat frogs and mice.

T F 13. Frogs can be housed in an aquarium.

T F 14. Toads enjoy eating rabbit pellets.

T F 15. Frogs enjoy small earthworms and insects.

T F 16. Canned dog food may be fed to toads.

T F 17. The pH balance can be made more acidic by adding sodium biphosphate.

T F 18. You can place a wooden box in one end of a rabbit cage for shelter.

T F 19. Cabbage and lettuce can be fed to fish.

T F 20. When rabbits have eaten cabbage, their urine has a strong, unpleasant odor.

Methods of Teaching Science

Activity D

Chapter 23

Name _____

Date _____ Period_____

You can use many objects, ideas, and events that are familiar to children to teach them science concepts. Listed below are the methods that were discussed in the chapter. List at least three science concepts that children could learn through each method of teaching.

1. Using color to teach science:_____

_____

_____

_____

_____

_____

2. Using water to teach science: _____

_____

_____

_____

_____

_____

3. Using foods to teach science: _____

_____

_____

_____

_____

_____

4. Using the child's own body to teach science: _____

_____

_____

_____

_____

_____

5. Using gardening to teach science:_____

_____

_____

_____

_____

_____

6. Using air to teach science:_____

_____

_____

_____

_____

7. Using magnets to teach science: _____
_____
_____
_____
_____

8. Using wheels to teach science: _____
_____
_____
_____
_____

9. Using field trips to teach science: _____
_____
_____
_____
_____

10. Using animals to teach science:_____
_____
_____
_____
_____

Guiding Social Studies Experiences  24

Social Studies Activities

Activity A   Name _____

Chapter 24   Date _____ Period_____

The early childhood years are an ideal time for children to begin learning about social studies. Young children can develop concepts related to each of the areas listed below. Describe one activity or incidental learning that would help promote learning in each area.

1. Develop self-respect and a healthy self-concept. _____
   _____
   _____
   _____
   _____

2. Develop respect for other people. _____
   _____
   _____
   _____
   _____

3. Develop self-control and independence. _____
   _____
   _____
   _____
   _____

4. Learn to share ideas and materials. _____
   _____
   _____
   _____
   _____

5. Develop healthy ways of relating to and working with others._____
   _____
   _____
   _____
   _____

(Continued)

6. Gain the attitudes, knowledge, and skills needed for living in a democracy. _____

_____

_____

_____

_____

7. Develop respect for other people's feelings, ideas, and property. _____

_____

_____

_____

_____

8. Learn about the roles people have in life. _____

_____

_____

_____

_____

9. Learn to appreciate the past and its relationship to the present. _____

_____

_____

_____

_____

10. Learn the need for and importance of rules. _____

_____

_____

_____

_____

Using a Theme in Planning

Name _____

Date _____ Period _____

Themes can be used to combine the learning opportunities of many different activities. Plan a social studies program around a theme of your choice. Describe several learning experiences for each of the activity areas listed.

Theme:	
Activity Area	**Learning Experience**
Art	
Field Trips	
Book Center	
Games	
Fingerplay	
Large Muscle Activity	
Cooking and Snacks	
Dramatic Play	
Small Manipulative	

Know Your Resources

Name _____

Date _____ Period _____

Identify available community resources that may be helpful in planning a variety of learning opportunities. Record the names of stores, museums, art galleries, community services, community workers, housing groups, and other community resources that may be helpful. List the information or services that each group can provide you. The Yellow Pages of your local telephone book is a good place to begin looking for this information.

Community Resources	Information/Services Provided

Guiding Food and Nutrition Experiences

Teaching Nutrition

Activity A   Name _____

Chapter 25   Date _____ Period_____

Develop a colorful rebus chart that presents basic nutrition information. In a rebus chart, basic drawings, symbols, or pictures are used in place of the words they represent. For example, the drawing  might replace the word *I*. Then describe how you would use this chart to explain the concepts to a group of young children.

How could you use this chart to explain nutrition concepts to a group of young children? _____

_____

_____

_____

_____

Collecting Recipes

Name _____

Date _____ Period _____

Research cookbooks and find two nutritious recipes that could be used with children. Write the recipes on the recipe cards provided. Beneath each recipe card, develop a recipe chart. Number each step on the chart and use very simple descriptions of the steps. Design the chart so young children will be able to follow along with your help.

Recipe: _____

Recipe Chart

(Continued)

Recipe: _____

Recipe Chart

Setting the Table

Name _____

Date _____ Period _____

Design a place mat for teaching children how to set the table. Include a plate, glass, fork, spoon, and napkin. Draw your place mat in the space provided. You can turn the page horizontally if you wish.

Guiding Music and Movement Experiences

26

Musical Truths

Activity A

Chapter 26

Name _____

Date _____ Period _____

Read the following statements about music. Circle *T* if the statement is true or *F* if the statement is false.

T F 1. Music is a form of communication.

T F 2. Music can be used to teach children language skills.

T F 3. Music experiences can help children build positive self-concepts.

T F 4. The music area should be located in a small corner of the classroom.

T F 5. Music experiences should always be structured.

T F 6. Teachers need to have loud singing voices.

T F 7. Children respond better to spoken directions than to musical directions.

T F 8. Music activities should be set in a time and place.

T F 9. The best songs for young children have a strongly defined mood or rhythm.

T F 10. Adding new words to a known melody is an easy way to make a song.

T F 11. The whole song method is best for teaching long songs.

T F 12. The teacher's enthusiasm and enjoyment of music are more important than a polished musical performance.

T F 13. The Autoharp® has several advantages over a piano.

T F 14. The guitar is easier to play than the Autoharp®.

T F 15. Rhythm instruments can be used to accompany the beat of a recording.

T F 16. If possible, use seven or eight types of rhythm instruments at one time.

T F 17. Children of all ages can enjoy sandpaper blocks.

T F 18. The children can take part in making rattlers.

T F 19. Children need to be taught how to listen.

T F 20. Movement activities are most successful when the children are tired and irritable.

Rhythm Instruments

Name _____

Date _____ Period _____

Choose one of the rhythm instruments listed below. Develop and perform a demonstration on how to make and use this instrument. Write your notes for the demonstration in the space provided.

sandpaper blocks	rattlers	tin can tom-toms
sandpaper sticks	shakers	coconut cymbals
bongo drums	rhythm sticks	jingle sticks
tom-tom drums	rhythm bells	

Instrument to be used: _____

Notes for demonstration: _____

_____

_____

_____

_____

_____

_____

_____

_____

_____

_____

_____

_____

_____

_____

_____

_____

_____

_____

_____

_____

_____

_____

_____

_____

Fingerplays

Activity C

Chapter 26

Name _____

Date _____ Period _____

List two considerations for choosing a fingerplay for a two-year-old.

1. _____

2. _____

In the space provided, write an original fingerplay that you could teach to a two-year-old child. Include descriptions of the actions that go along with the words.

_____

_____

_____

_____

_____

_____

_____

_____

_____

_____

_____

_____

_____

_____

_____

_____

_____

_____

_____

_____

_____

_____

_____

_____

_____

_____

_____

Teaching Movement

Name _____

Date _____ Period_____

Resolve each situation below by providing an appropriate solution.

1. You are going to teach children to clap with their hands. How can you do this?

   _____

   _____

   _____

2. You are assigned to teach a movement activity. How can you prepare for this?

   _____

   _____

   _____

3. One of the first movement activities should focus on listening. What type of beat should you provide for two-year-olds?

   _____

   _____

   _____

4. Space awareness is part of the preschool curriculum. How can you teach this concept?

   _____

   _____

   _____

5. You have been assigned to teach a word game. What types of words should you use?

   _____

   _____

   _____

6. You are planning a pantomiming activity. For what age level would this activity be most suitable?

   _____

   _____

   _____

Guiding Field Trip Experiences

Community Field Trips

Activity A

Chapter 27

Name _____

Date _____ Period _____

List 10 specific field trips in your community that young children would enjoy. List the themes that relate to each trip.

Field Trip	Related Themes
1.	
2.	
3.	
4.	
5.	
6.	
7.	
8.	
9.	
10.	

Planning the Trip

Name _____

Date _____ Period_____

Select one of the field trips from the list you created in Activity A. Fill in the information requested to make plans for the trip. Then trade your plans with another person and offer each other comments and suggestions for improving the plans.

Description of field trip selected: _____

_____

Age of children who will participate: _____

Number of children who will participate: _____

Number of adults who will help: _____

Ways children will learn through participation: _____

_____

_____

_____

_____

Total cost of the trip (including transportation, admission, food, etc.): _____

Time you will leave the center: _____

Approximate time you will return to the center: _____

Your educational goals for the trip: _____

_____

_____

_____

How you will prepare the children for the trip: _____

_____

_____

_____

Follow-up activities to reinforce learning: _____

_____

_____

_____

_____

Before and After the Field Trip

Activity C

Chapter 27

Name _____

Date _____ Period_____

The success of a field trip depends on how well the teacher prepares before the trip and follows up after the trip. Assume that you will be taking a group of children on a trip to the local post office. Brainstorm a list of specific pretrip preparations. Include plans you will make and information and questions to discuss with the tour guide prior to the field trip. Then brainstorm a list of follow-up activities to help children clarify their learning. Share your lists with others in the class.

Pretrip Preparations	**Follow-Up Activities**

Completing the Trip

Name _____

Date _____ Period_____

Complete the following statements about field trips by filling in the blanks with the correct words.

community	fall	observation	short
concepts	familiar	permission	social
crowds	file	preparation	theme
curriculum	follow-up	pretrip	tissues
directions	machinery	resource	value

_____ 1. Field trips are an important part of the _____ for preschool children.

_____ 2. Field trips help children develop _____ skills.

_____ 3. Vague _____ become clearer to children as they gain new information.

_____ 4. By participating in field trips children learn about their _____.

_____ 5. Taking field trips helps children practice following _____.

_____ 6. A field trip to the farm may be chosen while children are studying about farms, food, or _____.

_____ 7. A trip to a pumpkin patch or apple orchard can be taken during the _____ season.

_____ 8. The first trips children take should be _____ and nonthreatening.

_____ 9. After taking trips around the neighborhood, field trips may be taken to _____ places.

_____ 10. _____ walks provide a chance to sharpen children's observation skills.

_____ 11. People walks can teach many _____ concepts.

_____ 12. You should keep a _____ on field trips.

_____ 13. The success of a trip depends on your _____.

_____ 14. You should take paper _____ and a first aid kit on the trip.

_____ 15. _____ slips must be signed by parents.

_____ 16. _____ may overwhelm some children.

_____ 17. Guests or field trip hosts are called _____ people.

_____ 18. After setting goals for the trip, always take a _____ if you have never been to the trip site.

_____ 19. To help children clarify what they have learned, plan _____ activities.

_____ 20. Follow-up activities will reinforce the _____ of the experience.

Programs for Infants and Toddlers  28

Caregiver Traits

Activity A

Chapter 28

Name _____

Date _____ Period_____

Check all the traits listed that you feel an infant or toddler caregiver should model. Then go through the list again. This time check the traits you model. Answer the questions on the next page.

Personal Traits	Traits a Caregiver Should Model	Traits I Model	Personal Traits	Traits a Caregiver Should Model	Traits I Model
cheerful			disinterested		
forgetful			patient		
self-confident			friendly		
honest			shy		
cooperative			warm		
self-disciplined			cold		
unconfident			concerned		
curious			dependable		
active			enthusiastic		
nurturing			moody		
smiling			pleasant		
inflexible			helpful		
consistent			respectful		
reliable			predictable		
well-organized			kind		
trustworthy			understanding		
courteous			responsive		
unpredictable			easily distracted		

(Continued)

1. Compare your list of traits caregivers should model with the lists of others in the class. Did you choose the same traits? Why or why not? _____

   _____

   _____

   _____

   _____

   _____

2. In what general areas are you a model of positive traits? _____

   _____

   _____

   _____

   _____

   _____

3. In what areas can you improve? What can you do to improve? _____

   _____

   _____

   _____

   _____

   _____

4. Do you think a parent should model the same traits as a caregiver? Why or why not? _____

   _____

   _____

   _____

   _____

Environment Needs

Activity B

Chapter 28

Name _____

Date _____ Period_____

For each of the following questions, select the best answer and write the letter in the blank. Then give an explanation for each answer in the space provided.

_____ 1. The diapering area should be located next to a(n) _____.

        A. entrance   B. sink

Reason: _____

_____

_____ 2. In the feeding area, the floor surface should be _____.

        A. washable   B. carpeted

Reason: _____

_____

_____ 3. To prevent back strain for adults, _____-high changing surfaces should be used.

        A. hip   B. waist

Reason: _____

_____

_____ 4. The sleeping area should be adjacent to the _____ area.

        A. feeding   B. diapering

Reason: _____

_____

_____ 5. To create a separate play area for babies who crawl, _____ dividers should be used.

        A. low   B. high

Reason: _____

_____

_____ 6. In crowded areas toddlers are inclined to _____.

        A. cry   B. withdraw

Reason: _____

_____

_____ 7. A carpeted floor in the play area will be _____ for crawling children.

        A. warmer   B. uncomfortable

Reason: _____

_____

_____ 8. The sleeping area usually uses the _____ space.

      A. least   B. most

Reason: _____

_____

_____ 9. Infants _____ need a darkened room to sleep.

      A. do   B. do not

Reason: _____

_____

_____ 10. With infants and toddlers, routines are _____ time-consuming than with other preschool children.

      A. more   B. less

Reason: _____

_____

_____ 11. Toddlers need more _____ spaces than infants do.

      A. closed   B. open

Reason: _____

_____

_____ 12. The _____ area for toddlers should be located near the main entrance.

      A. receiving   B. diapering

Reason: _____

_____

_____ 13. Toddlers need one-third to _____ of the total classroom space open for play.

      A. one-half   B. three-fourths

Reason: _____

_____

_____ 14. Teachers of infants and toddlers usually prefer _____ flooring.

      A. tile   B. carpeted

Reason: _____

_____

_____ 15. The outdoor play areas should have a large, _____ area.

      A. paved   B. grassy

Reason: _____

_____

Toys for Development

Name _____

Date _____ Period_____

Clip pictures of toys from magazines or toy catalogs that promote fine motor, gross motor, reaching and grasping, and sound activities. Mount the pictures in the appropriate spaces. If pictures are unavailable, sketch the toys.

Fine Motor	Gross Motor
Reaching and Grasping	**Sounds**

Child Care Procedures

Name _____

Date _____ Period_____

The following story tells about Jan's first morning as an assistant in a child care center. Jan makes several mistakes. Read the story and find her errors. In the space provided, explain Jan's errors and tell what she should do in the future to avoid repeating the errors.

A New Job for Jan

Monday was Jan's first day assisting at the local child care center. She was thrilled to have gotten the job, and she began the day with enthusiasm.

Jan's first task was to greet parents and their children as they arrived in the receiving area. Five-month-old Timmy Henson began to cry as soon as Jan took him from his father. She quickly ran and placed him in a crib so she could greet other children. Surely Timmy would stop crying soon. Jan continued the morning by first reading a story to several children and then helping to supervise a painting activity.

Time was passing quickly, and Jan realized it was time for a diaper check. The infants were all awake except for Maria and Tom. Jan gently woke them. Tom did not need a change, but Maria was wet. Jan placed Maria on the floor and knelt down next to the crib to change her. Maria was crying, so Jan gave her a pacifier that she found on the floor. Maria was soon content.

As Jan was putting the clean diaper on Maria, she was called to help prepare the morning snack. Jan threw the dirty diaper in the garbage and wiped her hands on her pants. She picked up Maria and returned her to the crib to finish her nap.

Jan then went directly to the kitchen area where she began to cut up apples and cheese for the children's snack. She took the snack to the toddlers who were playing in the gross motor area. Jan was very tired after her busy morning, so she decided to take a break and read a magazine.

What mistakes did Jan make during her first morning on the job? What can she do to avoid making these mistakes in the future? _____

_____

_____

_____

_____

_____

_____

_____

_____

_____

_____

_____

_____

_____

_____

_____

_____

_____

Programs for School-Age Children  29

Quality School-Age Programs

Activity A

Chapter 29

Name _____

Date _____ Period _____

Read the following statements. Circle *Y* if the statement is characteristic of a quality school-age program. Circle *N* if it is not.

Y   N   1. Tailored to the needs, abilities, and interests of the children served.

Y   N   2. Mixed-age grouping is used to promote positive peer modeling and the development of leadership skills.

Y   N   3. Teachers use time out to discipline children.

Y   N   4. Schedules are rigid to teach children self-discipline.

Y   N   5. Children are allowed to help plan curriculum and make choices about activities.

Y   N   6. Environments are entirely designed to promote large group activities.

Y   N   7. Activities are designed to encourage the children to think, reason, question, and experiment.

Y   N   8. Activities foster a sense of dependence.

Y   N   9. Most staff-child interaction takes the form of instruction and verbal directions.

Y   N   10. Staff seek meaningful conversations with children.

Y   N   11. Staff recognize a child's efforts as well as accomplishments.

Y   N   12. A child's treatment by staff depends on the child's cultural background.

Y   N   13. Staff work with children to set clear limits.

Y   N   14. Motor activities focus on competitive games.

Y   N   15. A variety of materials is available for arts and crafts.

Y   N   16. Activities are designed to advance development.

Y   N   17. The reason for rules and expectations are explained to children.

Y   N   18. Staff include the children in problem-solving situations.

Y   N   19. Outdoor activities are limited to competitive games.

Y   N   20. Staff work in partnership with parents to meet each child's goals.

My Ideal Environment

Name _____

Date _____ Period _____

Pretend you are 10 years old. Your parents have arranged for you to attend an after-school program until they can pick you up at 5:30 each weekday evening. Describe your ideal environment for the center where you will be. Include both indoor (interest center, quiet areas, open areas) and outdoor space. Describe each area thoroughly, including floor coverings, wall coverings, furniture, and equipment. Keep in mind that this environment must meet the requirements of a quality school-age program.

Indoor Space

General description of my ideal indoor space:

Interest centers in my ideal center:

Quiet areas in my ideal center:

Open areas in my ideal center:

Outdoor Space

General description of my ideal outdoor space:

Design a Survey

Name _____

Date _____ Period _____

Design a survey to be used with school-age children to assess their interests. This information would be used to plan the curriculum for an after-school program. Begin by choosing a title for your survey. Then include the questions or incomplete sentences that you would use in the survey.

Title: _____

_____

_____

_____

_____

_____

_____

_____

_____

_____

_____

_____

_____

_____

_____

_____

_____

_____

_____

_____

_____

_____

_____

_____

_____

_____

_____

_____

_____

_____

_____

Games for Fostering Development

Name _____

Date _____ Period_____

In a small group, brainstorm a list of games that school-age children would enjoy and that would also foster development: physical, cognitive, emotional, or social. List the games under one of the four categories shown below: board, card, indoor, or outdoor games. Then indicate the type of development each would foster.

Board Games	
Name	Type of Development

Outdoor Games	
Name	Type of Development

Card Games	
Name	Type of Development

Indoor Games	
Name	Type of Development

Guiding Children with Special Needs  30

Special Needs Match

Activity A

Chapter 30

Name _____

Date _____ Period _____

Match the following terms and definitions.

_____ 1. Is illustrated when a speaker uses a variety of pitches and loudness levels during routine conversation

_____ 2. An illness that persists over a period of time.

_____ 3. An individual learning plan designed for each child with special needs.

_____ 4. A severe hearing loss that causes a child to have little understandable speech.

_____ 5. Related to the amount of energy or volume used when speaking.

_____ 6. Chemicals or drugs injected into the body.

_____ 7. An artificial limb.

_____ 8. Things that contact the body through touch.

_____ 9. Term used for placing children with special needs in a regular classroom.

_____ 10. Type of epileptic seizure that causes a child to lose consciousness and jerk, thrash, or become stiff.

_____ 11. Technique that involves taking a child's mispronounced words and correctly using them in sentences.

_____ 12. The lowness or highness of the voice.

_____ 13. Having a physical disability but being able to move from place to place.

_____ 14. Food, drugs, or anything taken through the mouth.

_____ 15. Process in which a child who is gifted is assigned to a class with older children.

_____ 16. Process in which the range of experiences is broadened to provide the child with a special curriculum.

_____ 17. Type of epileptic seizure that may go unnoticed.

_____ 18. Airborne substances that are inhaled.

_____ 19. Having exceptional skill in one of the following areas: creative or productive thinking, general intellectual ability, psychomotor ability, leadership ability, specific academic aptitudes, visual or performing arts.

A. acceleration

B. ambulatory

C. chronic health need

D. contactants

E. enrichment

F. expansion

G. giftedness

H. grand mal seizure

I. Individualized Educational Plan (IEP)

J. ingestants

K. inhalants

L. injectables

M. loudness

N. mainstreaming

O. petit mal seizure

P. pitch

Q. profound hearing loss

R. prosthesis

S. voice flexibility

Special Communication Needs

Activity B

Chapter 30

Name _____

Date _____ Period _____

To reinforce your understanding of the communication problems children with special needs may have, answer the following questions.

1. How can you identify a child who is hearing impaired? _____

   _____

   _____

   _____

2. What treatment is often used for children who are hearing impaired? _____

   _____

   _____

   _____

3. What are some suggestions for teaching children who are hearing impaired? _____

   _____

   _____

   _____

   _____

4. What are articulation problems? _____

   _____

   _____

5. How can a teacher help children who have articulation problems? _____

   _____

   _____

   _____

6. What can a teacher do to create good speaking conditions for children who stutter? _____

   _____

   _____

   _____

7. What is amblyopia? _____

   _____

   _____

   _____

8. How is amblyopia treated? _____

   _____

   _____

(Continued)

9. What is glaucoma? _____

_____

_____

_____

_____

10. How is glaucoma treated? _____

_____

_____

_____

11. What is the difference between nearsightedness and farsightedness? _____

_____

_____

_____

_____

12. Explain color deficiency. _____

_____

_____

_____

13. List at least three ways a teacher can help children who have visual disabilities. _____

_____

_____

_____

Physical and Health Disorders

Activity C

Chapter 30

Name _____

Date _____ Period_____

Explain each of the following disorders and describe problems that a child with each disorder would face.

Allergies	
Amputation	
Arthritis	
Asthma	
Cerebral palsy	
Cystic fibrosis	
Diabetes	
Epilepsy	
Hemophilia	
Leukemia	
Spina bifida	

Helping Children Who Have Special Needs

Activity D

Chapter 30

Name _____

Date _____ Period_____

Read a magazine or newspaper article that relates to teaching children with special needs in an inclusionary class-room. Write a report in the space provided. Then summarize what you feel are the most important considerations for teachers and what you learned from the article. Share this information orally with the class.

Title of article:_____

Source of article:_____

Report:_____

Summary comments (important considerations for teachers of children with special needs and what you learned from reading the article):_____

_____

_____

_____

_____

_____

_____

_____

_____

_____

_____

_____

_____

_____

_____

_____

_____

_____

_____

_____

_____

_____

_____

_____

The Child Who Is Gifted

Name _____

Date _____ Period _____

Interview a parent or teacher of a young child who has been identified as gifted to learn more about how to handle this special need. Ask the following questions.

What is the child's age? _____

In what area(s) is the child gifted? _____

_____

_____

How was the child identified as gifted? _____

_____

_____

What characteristics identify the child as being gifted? _____

_____

_____

_____

_____

What special programs have been made available at home, at school, and in the community to help meet the needs of the child who is gifted? _____

_____

_____

_____

Use the space below for more specific questions and answers related to the child you are studying.

_____

_____

_____

_____

_____

_____

_____

_____

_____

_____

_____

Getting Parents Involved

Activity A

Chapter 31

Name _____

Date _____ Period_____

Complete each of the following sentences using the correct word or words.

active   newsletters   problem-solving file

daily news flash   orientation   professional

debating   parent involvement   reinforcement

educational   planning   sunshine call

letters   positive   theme

_____ 1. A telephone call made by a teacher to a parent to communicate praise and support for the child is referred to as a _____.

_____ 2. Your writing style in a newsletter should match the _____ level of the parents.

_____ 3. _____ refers to patterns of participation in educational programs by parents.

_____ 4. To have a successful parent-teacher conference, you must first spend time _____.

_____ 5. When you use a parent's name in conversation to improve your memory, you are using the process of _____.

_____ 6. A letter or newsletter should be written using the _____ voice.

_____ 7. Information on problems parents may face can be organized into a _____.

_____ 8. Teachers get the most from parent volunteers when they provide a(n) _____ session.

_____ 9. The _____ is a written communication for parents that contains news about events and occasions at the center.

_____ 10. Letters sent to parents often include the _____ of the week.

_____ 11. _____ are written communications that often address only one subject and are put out on an "as needed" basis.

_____ 12. It is best to begin and end the parent-teacher conference with a _____ comment.

_____ 13. A problem that often occurs in group discussions is that groups begin _____ among themselves.

_____ 14. When meeting with parents, the teacher should always model _____ behavior.

_____ 15. _____ are written communications that include information concerning a variety of topics and are put out on a regular basis.

Parent Letters

Name _____

Date _____ Period_____

Assume you are a teacher and have been asked to write the first letter of the year to parents. Write a letter in the active voice that includes the following information:

- An introduction of yourself and the other teachers.

- Classroom goals, rules, and expectations.

- An invitation to parents to observe and/or take part in the classroom.

_____

_____

_____

_____

_____

_____

_____

_____

_____

_____

_____

_____

_____

_____

_____

_____

_____

_____

_____

_____

_____

_____

_____

_____

_____

_____

_____

_____

_____

_____

_____

_____

Parent Discussion Groups

Activity C

Chapter 31

Name _____

Date _____ Period_____

In the chart below, list advantages and disadvantages of using discussion groups for teaching parenting information. Then use the chart to answer the questions that follow. Discuss your answers in class.

Advantages of Discussion Groups	Disadvantages of Discussion Groups

1. What do you think is the strongest argument in favor of using parent discussion? _____

_____

_____

_____

_____

(Continued)

2. Why might some parents dislike discussion groups? _____

_____

_____

_____

_____

_____

_____

3. What do you think is the strongest argument against using parent discussion groups? Why? _____

_____

_____

_____

_____

_____

_____

_____

Teacher Hotline

Name _____

Date _____ Period_____

Pretend you are an advice columnist who writes a "Teacher Hotline" column for an educational journal. Answer the following letters from teachers about their concerns in working with parents.

Dear Teacher Hotline:

I have difficulty working with parents. For some reason, when I point out the family's weaknesses, the parents get defensive. What should I do?

Signed,
A Discouraged Teacher

Dear Discouraged Teacher:

_____

_____

_____

_____

_____

_____

_____

Sincerely,
T.H.

Dear Teacher Hotline:

My director has asked me to publish a newsletter. I am afraid to confess that I do not know what to include in the newsletter. What should I do? Help!

Signed,
A Confused Teacher

Dear Confused Teacher:

_____

_____

_____

_____

_____

_____

_____

Sincerely,
T.H.

Dear Teacher Hotline,

Whenever parents visit my classroom, I feel uncomfortable. My pulse increases and I feel nervous. How can I relax?

Signed,
An Uncomfortable Teacher

Dear Uncomfortable Teacher:

_____

_____

_____

_____

_____

_____

_____

Sincerely,
T.H.

Dear Teacher Hotline,

Last Tuesday I began my job as a head teacher in a new center. My director has asked me to write the first parent letter. My concern is how to make parent letters interesting. Can you help?

Signed,
A Questioning Teacher

Dear Questioning Teacher:

_____

_____

_____

_____

_____

_____

_____

Sincerely,
T.H.

(Continued)

Dear Teacher Hotline:

How important are first impressions? Last week I had my first parent-teacher conference. Without thinking I told a parent that his child was a brat. The father got angry and walked out. Now what do I do?
Signed,
Out of Answers

Dear Out of Answers:

_____

_____

_____

_____

_____

_____

_____

Sincerely,
T.H.

Dear Teacher Hotline:

I am embarrassed that I don't know what to do! On Thursday I had a conference with a timid parent. This mother couldn't even hold eye contact with me. We scheduled a continuation of the conference next week. How can I make the mother feel more comfortable?
Signed,
Embarrassed

Dear Embarrassed:

_____

_____

_____

_____

_____

_____

_____

Sincerely,
T.H.

Dear Teacher Hotline:

The staff at my school are having a difficult time scheduling parent-teacher conferences. We are allowed to use the time from 4 to 5 p.m. for this activity three days a month. What should we do?
Signed,
No Answers

Dear No Answers:

_____

_____

_____

_____

_____

_____

_____

Sincerely,
T.H.

Dear Teacher Hotline:

I am working with a parent who insists that I spank his child. How can I convince this father that spanking isn't successful?
Sincerely,
Opposed

Dear Opposed:

_____

_____

_____

_____

_____

_____

_____

Sincerely,
T.H.

A Career for You in Child Care  32

Know How to Job Hunt

Activity A

Chapter 32

Name _____

Date _____ Period_____

Decide whether the following statements about job hunting are true or false. Circle *T* if the statement is true or *F* if the statement is false.

T F 1. Completing a budget will help you determine your minimum take-home pay requirements.

T F 2. Recent graduates should not list lab work or volunteer work in their field of study on a resume.

T F 3. The ideal time to ask about vacations is during your interview.

T F 4. In nearly all interviews, applicants are given the opportunity to ask questions.

T F 5. A brief thank-you note sent soon after an interview is a basic courtesy that serves as a reminder to those you met.

T F 6. Keeping a mental record of each cover letter you send is sufficient.

T F 7. You should try to state success incidents and accomplishments in your interview.

T F 8. Asking questions of your supervisor and fellow employees will help you learn more about your job and improve your skills.

T F 9. Interviewers cannot legally ask certain questions because they may be discriminatory.

T F 10. A resume is a brief summary of your qualifications, skills, and job experiences.

T F 11. You should not make a list of jobs you would enjoy because this limits your employment options.

T F 12. The hidden job market involves jobs that are advertised informally through word of mouth.

T F 13. When employers evaluate a resume, they look for gaps in employment dates, the amount of space given to earlier jobs, and the emphasis on education.

T F 14. Newspapers list all job titles related to child care under "child care teacher."

T F 15. As long as you have sent a resume in advance, you do not need to take a resume to the interview.

T F 16. You should be careful not to volunteer negative information about former employers or yourself during an interview.

T F 17. When interviewers ask about your weaknesses, answer as quickly as possible and then change the subject.

T F 18. Reading newspaper ads once a week is more efficient than reading them every day.

T F 19. Being involved in professional organizations does little to help in the job search.

T F 20. Your resume may serve as your own self-inventory.

Career Preferences

Name _____

Date _____ Period_____

Rank the following jobs in order of your preference with 1 being the most preferable and 11 being the least preferable.

_____ infant teacher

_____ toddler teacher

_____ preschool teacher

_____ child care teacher

_____ Montessori teacher

_____ teacher in parent cooperative

_____ teacher's aide

_____ center director

_____ assistant director

_____ kindergarten teacher

_____ assistant kindergarten teacher

What aspects of your top three choices do you find most appealing? _____

_____

_____

_____

_____

What special skills could you apply to your top three choices?_____

_____

_____

_____

_____

What aspects of your bottom three choices do you find least appealing? _____

_____

_____

_____

_____

A Job Application

Complete the following job application form. When you are finished, divide into small groups and evaluate one another's applications.

Community Child Care Center

NAME AND ADDRESS

First Name	Middle Name	Last Name	Social Security No.	Date of Application

PERMANENT MAILING ADDRESS				TELEPHONE NO.
Number and street		City	State Zip code	(Area) Local Number

Are you over 18 years of age and less than 70?

JOB INTEREST

Title of position for which you are applying:

Full-Time ☐   Part-Time ☐   Permanent ☐   Temporary ☐   Summer ☐

Are you currently employed?   Yes ☐   No ☐   Date available to start:

EDUCATION AND TRAINING

Name and Address (City & State) of last Grade School Attended	Dates Attended	Major Studies	Did You Graduate? Yes ☐ No ☐

Name and Address (City & State) of last High School Attended	Dates Attended	Major Studies	Did You Graduate? Yes ☐ No ☐

Name and Address (City & State) of Business Career or Technical School Attended	Dates Attended	Major Studies	Did You Graduate? Yes ☐ No ☐

COLLEGE LEVEL AND ABOVE (Including Junior & Community Colleges)				
SCHOOL NAME	SCHOOL LOCATION (City & State)	DATE GRADUATED (or Years attended) Month/Year	TYPE OF DEGREE RECEIVED	MAJOR & MINOR FIELD OF STUDY

Your College Grade Point Average =
A =   Lowest Passing =

Awards or Honors:

Special Skills:

Professional Memberships related to the position:

(Continued)

Name _____

EMPLOYMENT RECORD

Please list every employer, including part-time. Begin with your present or most recent employer.

Date	Name & Address—Employer	1 Position or Occupation 2 Department 3 Name of supervisor	Describe Major Duties	Salary or Wages (Monthly)	Reason for leaving
From 　Month/Year To 　Month/Year		1 2 3		Starting $_____ Final $_____	
From 　Month/Year To 　Month/Year		1 2 3		Starting $_____ Final $_____	
From 　Month/Year To 　Month/Year		1 2 3		Starting $_____ Final $_____	
From 　Month/Year To 　Month/Year		1 2 3		Starting $_____ Final $_____	

REFERENCES (do not list relatives)

Name	Address	Phone No.	Occupation	Years Known

ADDITIONAL DATA

Have you ever been convicted of a crime (other than traffic or other minor violations)　Yes ☐　No ☐ that would affect your job performance?

If yes, give nature of offence and other circumstances regarding conviction.

Are you a U.S. citizen?　　　　　　　　　　　　　　　　　　　　　Yes ☐　No ☐
If "No," do you have an alien registration card or valid U.S. work permit?　Yes ☐　No ☐

Non-English languages you read　　　　　　speak　　　　　　　　　write

Other special skills, knowledges and abilities which support your qualifications for the position you are seeking:

PHYSICAL STATUS

Do you have any disabilities that would affect your job performance?　　Yes ☐　No ☐
If yes, explain:

In completing, and submitting this application, I understand and agree: That any misstatement of material facts will be sufficient reason for immediate withdrawal of this application or, in the event of employment be deemed cause for dismissal. That my previous employers may be asked for information concerning my employment, character, ability, and experiences. That no question on this application has been answered in such a manner as to disclose my race, religion, or national origin. That if employed, I may be required to furnish proof of age by birth or baptismal certificate.

Signature _____　Date of Application _____

The Bottom Line

Name _____

Date _____ Period _____

Becoming a full-time member of the workforce involves becoming financially responsible for yourself. Before you accept a position, you will want to know whether the salary offered will meet your financial needs. Completing the budget below will provide you with this information.

A Monthly Budget		
	"Rock Bottom" $ Spent Per Month	"I Wish" $ Spent Per Month
I. Necessities		
food	_____	_____
housing	_____	_____
utilities	_____	_____
transportation	_____	_____
personal care	_____	_____
health care	_____	_____
clothing	_____	_____
insurance	_____	_____
other: _____	_____	_____
Subtotal I:	_____	_____
II. Extras		
entertainment	_____	_____
recreation	_____	_____
gifts and contributions	_____	_____
savings	_____	_____
education	_____	_____
other: _____	_____	_____
Subtotal II:	_____	_____
III. Taxes and Social Security		
Add 30 percent of Subtotal I + Subtotal II	_____	_____
Subtotal III:	_____	_____
IV. Miscellaneous		
Add 20 percent of Subtotal I + Subtotal II	_____	_____
Subtotal IV:	_____	_____
V: Total		
Subtotal I	_____	_____
Subtotal II	_____	_____
Subtotal III	_____	_____
Subtotal IV	_____	_____
Total:	_____	_____

166

Lesson Plan Form

Name _____

Date _____ **Period** _____

Group: _____

Name of Activity: _____

Date scheduled: _____ Time scheduled: _____

Goals: _____

_____

_____

_____

_____

_____

_____

_____

Learning objectives: _____

_____

_____

_____

_____

_____

Materials needed: _____

_____

_____

_____

_____

_____

Motivation/introduction: _____

_____

_____

_____

_____

_____

_____

(Continued)

Name _____

Procedures: _____

_____

_____

_____

_____

_____

_____

_____

Closure/transition: _____

_____

_____

_____

_____

Evaluation: _____

_____

_____

_____

_____

_____

Lesson Plan Form

Name _____

Date _____ **Period** _____

Group: _____

Name of Activity: _____

Date scheduled: _____ Time scheduled: _____

Goals: _____

_____

_____

_____

_____

_____

_____

_____

Learning objectives: _____

_____

_____

_____

_____

_____

Materials needed: _____

_____

_____

_____

_____

_____

Motivation/introduction: _____

_____

_____

_____

_____

_____

_____

(Continued)

Procedures: _____

_____

_____

_____

_____

_____

_____

_____

Closure/transition: _____

_____

_____

_____

_____

Evaluation: _____

_____

_____

_____

_____

_____

Lesson Plan Form

Name _____

Date _____ **Period**_____

Group: _____

Name of Activity: _____

Date scheduled: _____Time scheduled: _____

Goals:_____

_____

_____

_____

_____

_____

_____

_____

Learning objectives: _____

_____

_____

_____

_____

_____

Materials needed: _____

_____

_____

_____

_____

_____

Motivation/introduction: _____

_____

_____

_____

_____

_____

_____

(Continued)

Procedures: _____

_____

_____

_____

_____

_____

_____

_____

Closure/transition: _____

_____

_____

_____

_____

Evaluation: _____

_____

_____

_____

_____

_____

Lesson Plan Form

Name _____

Date _____ **Period** _____

Group: _____

Name of Activity: _____

Date scheduled: _____Time scheduled: _____

Goals:_____

_____

_____

_____

_____

_____

_____

_____

Learning objectives: _____

_____

_____

_____

_____

_____

Materials needed: _____

_____

_____

_____

_____

_____

Motivation/introduction: _____

_____

_____

_____

_____

_____

_____

(Continued)

Name _____

Procedures: _____

_____

_____

_____

_____

_____

_____

_____

_____

Closure/transition: _____

_____

_____

_____

_____

Evaluation:_____

_____

_____

_____

_____

_____

_____

Lesson Plan Form

Name _____

Date _____ **Period** _____

Group: _____

Name of Activity: _____

Date scheduled: _____ Time scheduled: _____

Goals: _____

_____

_____

_____

_____

_____

_____

_____

_____

Learning objectives: _____

_____

_____

_____

_____

_____

Materials needed: _____

_____

_____

_____

_____

_____

Motivation/introduction: _____

_____

_____

_____

_____

_____

_____

(Continued)

Name _____

Procedures: _____

_____

_____

_____

_____

_____

_____

_____

_____

Closure/transition: _____

_____

_____

_____

_____

Evaluation: _____

_____

_____

_____

_____

_____